Demystifying
the Monologue

Demystifying the Monologue

Your

Road Map

to a

Compelling

Performance

Leonard Peters

HEINEMANN
Portsmouth, NH

Heinemann

A division of Reed Elsevier Inc.

361 Hanover Street

Portsmouth, NH 03801–3912

www.heinemanndrama.com

Offices and agents throughout the world

The author and publisher wish to thank those who have generously given permission to reprint borrowed material:

Excerpt from *The Rose Tattoo* by Tennessee Williams, from *The Theatre of Tennessee Williams*, Vol. II, copyright © 1950 by The University of the South. Renewed 1978 by The University of the South. Reprinted by permission of New Directions Publishing Corp.

Acknowledgment of borrowed material continues on page 204.

Library of Congress Cataloging-in-Publication Data

Peters, Leonard.

    Demystifying the monologue: your road map to a compelling performance / Leonard Peters.

        p. cm.

    ISBN 0-325-00764-0 (alk. paper)

    1. Monologues. 2. Acting. I. Title.

    PN2080.P48 2005

    792.02'8—dc22   2005022434

Editor: Lisa A. Barnett

Production coordinator: Elizabeth Valway

Production management: Matrix Productions

Typesetter: Argosy

Cover design: Joni Doherty

Manufacturing: Steve Bernier

Printed in the United States of America on acid-free paper

10 09 08 07 06 VP 1 2 3 4 5

For Sylvia

who
Believed indefatigably
Supported indomitably
Loved unconditionally

"Carpe Diem!!!"

Contents

Acknowledgments

Writing a book is not something one does by oneself, although sitting at the keyboard is done alone. The information presented in this book has come from many sources and people. I want to acknowledge them for their contribution.

First and foremost, I thank the actors, the ones I watched, directed, taught, and coached over the years. Each one taught me something. I am grateful for the intensive education. Here, too, I want to thank Michael Shurtleff who many years ago introduced me to teaching.

I want to acknowledge the support of Steve Brand, Katherine Crowley, Eric Jennings, Eric Head, Carrie Maher and Mark Greenwald, Alvin Deutsch, Barbara Field, and Susan Dworkin. Special thanks to Ginny Read, the first person to encourage me to write this book.

I want to thank Karen De Mauro and Julie Boak for their unconditional support and belief, and Jerry Mundis for his own special participation. A special thank you to Judith Ivey for all the time, scrutiny, and kind words she said about this book. Three people, Ron Drummond, Peter Francis James, and David Chandler, have my undying gratitude. They worked far beyond the call of friendship, offering insightful and specific thoughts.

A very appreciative thank you to Michael Shepley, without whom this book might never have been born.

To my agent, Bob Silverstein, for being there. To my editor, Lisa A. Barnett, whose patience and belief brought this book to fulfillment. Thank you both.

Thank you is also due to Elizabeth Valway, Aaron Downey, Melissa Woods, and Eric Chalek for their various contributions. Most importantly to Ann Whetstone for her excellent green pencil work and her suggestions and ideas that contributed to the clarity, specificity, and realization of the book.

Last, but by no means least, I thank Nydia Leaf who acted as a second pair of eyes when mine were crossed and bloodshot. And I have a special place for the four writers whose material offered me so much richness.

Introduction

Over the three decades I have worked with actors as director, coach, and teacher, performing monologues has created the greatest angst, blind spots, and feigned lack of understanding. I say "feigned" because when being confronted with performing a monologue, whether in a production or for an audition, the actors' knowledge of their craft evaporates and is replaced by fear, confusion, and uncertainty. Monologues appear to be one big mystery.

"A monologue?" "Why does anyone want to see a monologue?" "How do I find the right monologue?" "Everything I've learned is about creating a relationship with another person. A monologue presents a character talking to himself or talking to an invisible person." "Where do I begin?" "Who am I talking to?" "What am I doing?" "How do I use what I know about acting when acting alone?" "Help me!!!"

These questions, along with the cries for help from both students and professional actors, prompted me to write this book to lift the veil of confusion, ease the actor's and student's angst, and demystify the mystery monologues create.

Demystifying the Monologue addresses the issue of monologue mysteries by using actor's tools, character-fulfilling needs, and various script and character analyses that offer simple, specific answers in a focused, connect-the-dots premise culminating in a practical road map. This road map replaces fear and anxiety with clarity and confidence, guiding any actor to a fully realized character delivering a compelling monologue. The road map is a useful guide for all future work with monologues.

First, let me clear up a major misconception about monologues. A character delivering a monologue is not acting alone. A monologue is a dialogue between two people. One person speaking, the other listening and reacting, creating a relationship between the two. The other person, the listener, is the more important of the two characters because he holds the key to helping a character achieve his objective.

There is more to performing a monologue than just making a selection, learning the words, and performing. What is often overlooked is creating the character who is delivering the monologue. When performing a monologue, whether for ninety seconds or two hours, you need to create the characters and the entire world they inhabit. You create this world using your senses, intellect, awareness, and insight, including your ability to create relationships interpreted from your personally chosen material. Once you inhabit this world, your character will not be acting alone.

Demystifying the Monologue guides you step by step through the creative process of building a fully realized human being in a sensorily alive environment, performing a rich and compelling monologue.

The fear and responsibility of performing alone creates anxiety, mystery, and confusion. The need to excite and interest an audience by taking them on an emotional journey while talking to an unseen person can cause panic, preventing you from remaining open to your process and accessing your basic knowledge of the craft of acting.

Demystification begins with a simple understanding. If you can create an organic, fully realized, three-dimensional human being alive in the moment, you can create a complex character delivering a compelling monologue. This step-by-step process will replace your fear of monologues with the enjoyment you experience when acting with another person.

When you're alone, do you talk to yourself? Do you expect an answer? Guidance? To be offered peace and serenity? Help in clearing up your immediate need? Is there another person? Is that person real to you in that moment? Do you believe the person can give you what you need? Do you feel that other person is there with you? Is it an imaginary person, or do you know her?

Of course that person is real in the moment. You are in a dialogue with her or him. The other person is listening and reacting to you, prompting you to continue talking even though no one is talking back. You may not be allowing them to respond. The other person offers you what you need emotionally in that moment to get to the next moment.

A monologue expresses your work. Work made up of committed choices. Choices of monologue, interpretation, objective, and the relationship created with the other person. These fulfilled choices and decisions give insights into the unique awareness you bring to the creation of your character. You communicate a personal perspective of human psychological understanding, taking the audience on an individual and emotionally complex journey that compels it to travel with you.

Acting is communicating. You communicate your character's need for understanding and love. Keeping your character in the moment and sharing his or her struggle with the audience involves it in your character's needs. Involving the audience in understanding your character's human needs compels it to root for you to achieve your objective.

Trusting your choices and decisions brings commitment to your work. The road map aids you in believing in your choices by giving you a foundation on which to build your character. Your work is made up of choices and decisions. Every decision needs to be thought out and specifically chosen. In life, you can be arbitrary. In your work, every choice and every decision need to be carefully explored. Trust your choices. You made them. Trust the material. You chose it. Your interpretation is derived from your personal perspective. Everything you bring to your character is uniquely yours. Trust your instinct to bring you to your personal truth of interpretation.

Artists struggle with each choice of color, brush, and stroke. Musicians with notes, chords, and tempi. Writers with each word, syntax, and tense. You with choices, decisions, and specificity. Interpretation creates a personal struggle. This is where your instinct comes into play. Trust what you see, feel, taste, touch, and smell. Everything else is fleeting. An idea is momentary. What you sense is your truth. Your mind can play games on you. Your senses never lie. They know your truth because they are you. They create your aesthetic: your likes, dislikes, loves, hates, enjoyments. Your senses are the universals that bring you together with your audience. Everyone feels the same but thinks differently. Trust your instinct. It is your true guiding factor.

Acting is subjective. This very fact makes it difficult to trust yourself. The need to be within the character, finding the root of your character's spine, needs, and motivation, causes you to lose perspective. Trusting your instinct frees you to perceive the material from the character's perspective. Believing the circumstance, situation, other characters, and moments from the viewpoint of your character helps you get inside and interpret the material from a wholly subjective place. This subjectivity creates your own personal and original interpretation of your character. Totally accepting your character's situation and circumstance offers you the freedom to trust and experience your instinct in creating the character.

Characters are subjective in their own lives and often do not see what others observe of them. Any given text offers clues for the actor to discover and use in the understanding and building of a character. Plumbing the text carefully directs you to making truthful and specific decisions for the honesty of your character.

Commitment to the character's world, beliefs, and perspective is key. Giving yourself over to your chosen decisions creates spontaneity and carries the audience moment by moment through your monologue. The more specifically you believe in your character, the easier and stronger your commitment. Turning yourself over to and inhabiting your character's need for taking her moment-to-moment emotional journey creates a person fully living each moment for the first time.

Monologues are not new to theatre. With the resurgence of one-person plays, monologue-compiled evenings, and monodramas, *Demystifying the Monologue* offers insight and guidance to all creative and interpretative artists involved in these endeavors. It addresses the needs of creating the character and fulfilling his monologue, and offers useful guidelines to actors, writers, and directors of monodramas and monologue-compiled evenings, as well as singers for their cabaret evenings.

Singers compile songs for a variety-filled evening's cabaret performance. They learn the songs musically and then proceed to the meaning of the lyrics. The songs are strung together by the point of view, or objective, they communicate to the audience. An evening of songs is comparable to an evening's compilation of monologues. The principles in *Demystifying the Monologue* guide the singer to a personal and involving interpretation of the lyrics. After all, what is a song but a monologue set to music.

Performing a monologue showcases both your knowledge of creating a character and performing. When fulfilled, it is the quintessence of the art of acting. Two powerfully realized solo performances have been honored with Tony awards: Christopher Plummer's *Barrymore* and Jefferson Mays' *I Am My Own Wife*.

What are these theatre pieces if not monologues extended to a full evening's experience? Monodramas and monologue-compiled evenings are very old forms of theatre. Artists have often appeared in them to showcase their work. Sarah Bernhardt toured in an evening of highlights from her greatest performances. Ruth Draper, a celebrated monologist of her day, transformed the dramatic "monologue" *The Italian Lesson* from parlor entertainment into high art, touring with it for more than three decades. In this fully realized play, she portrayed multiple characters, populating the stage with a completely believable supporting cast.

More recently, Lily Tomlin used her unique talent to perform in two one-person plays, *The Search for Signs of Intelligent Life in the Universe* and *Appearing Nitely*, both authored by Jane Wagner. John Leguizamo wrote and appeared in *Mambo Mouth* and *Freaks*. Sir John Gielgud, in *Ages of Man,* turned an evening of Shakespearean monologues into a highly successful tour de force. Susannah York appeared in *The Loves of Shakespeare's Women,* and Judith Ivey created thirteen different people in *Women on Fire* by Irene O'Garden.

Writers have also created one-person dramas with great success. In 1930, Jean Cocteau wrote *La Voix Humaine,* a play that has been performed by Ingrid Bergman, Anna Magnani, Luise Rainer, Gertrude Lawrence, and Flora Robson. Doug Wright's *I Am My Own Wife* won both the Pulitzer Prize for Drama and the Tony Award for Best New Play.

Using four speeches by well-known dramatists—William Shakespeare, Tennessee Williams, Lorraine Hansberry, and Wendy Wasserstein, *Demystifying the Monologue* illustrates a comprehensive technique for creating a fully realized, complex character performing a compelling monologue. Encompassing a variety of language and styles, the book describes, clearly and simply, the purpose of each element needed to develop the four characters. Every aspect will be discussed for each character, explaining in subtly different ways how to look at and think about evolving a character's life. This step-by-step process offers you a road map to explain how to turn theory into practice.

Creating four characters delivering four monologues may appear to be repetitive, but each is an additional way of looking at and using the actor's tools and each specific character's need. Over the years, I have found myself offering slightly different interpretations of thoughts and ideas to actors and students only to have them come to understand by these subtle alterations. In most cases, the seeming repetition clears up the confusion they were having with a particular aspect in their work.

Sometimes over months, sometimes years, what appears to be repetition provides subtle differences in comprehending and utilizing each aspect in the creation of your character. If you think you immediately understand, explore the remainder with fresh eyes. See what more you may learn in order to enlarge your range for using the actor's tools and character's need for each of the following characters and their monologues.

Creating each specific character requires a different investigation, thereby using the tools in specifically different ways for each character's particular emotional makeup and truth. Look carefully into each because making your decisions can be subtly different while appearing the same. These subtle differences are what make each character different and personal. Characters will use more or less of certain tools because each has different needs to be fulfilled. One of the characters may use less of one tool then another. If you examine all four, you will reach a clearer understanding of the practical use and importance of each piece needed for fulfilling the life of your character.

Exploring the use of the actor's tools along with the character's needs creates an emotionally layered human being. The layering creates complexity, variety, mystery, and surprise, giving you a wide range of choices to use in your interpretation. Understanding the important need for the other person turns the monologue into a dialogue between two people talking, listening, behaving, and reacting to one another. Shaping the monologue into a three-act play with a beginning, middle, and end aids in specifically evolving the character's emotional journey.

At the same time, the greater your understanding of each tool and character need, the more variety you will bring to the development of your character, offering you the widest variety of choices. This variety makes each of your characters different and specific unto himself.

Demystifying the Monologue presents a road map for performing compelling monologues, monodramas, and monologue-compiled theatre pieces. It is an invaluable book for actors, writers, directors, singers, students, teachers, instructors, professors, amateur theatre groups, and people who just plain love good acting.

1

Choosing a Monologue

Choosing a monologue is a daunting task. There is an abundance of material available from plays, movies, novels, speeches, and other sources. Monologues showcase your work. They illustrate your understanding of human behavior and display your depth of knowledge of your craft.

Everything begins with a choice. A writer with a word. A musician with a note. A painter with a brush, color, or canvas. An actor chooses a person to bring to life. Every choice is yours and expresses you.

Choices are key to your personal interpretation of a character and his monologue. As you proceed step by step, your work becomes a series of personally felt and committed choices. It reveals your unique voice, insight, and understanding of humanity. Nothing is arbitrary. The more specific your choices, the greater your freedom and the spontaneity to fulfill them.

Examine your personal choices. Awaken to your needs and perceptions that led you to making your personal life choices. Each of these needs must be explored for your character's evolution. Where you are in your life today is a choice. You chose to be an actor. You chose your friends. If you think this was happenstance, look deeper. Somewhere in the whole of your life's experience you will discover, sense, and understand your decisions. Where you live, your clothes, personal style, and persona are all decided-upon choices arrived at over time and often through particular situations and circumstances. Your religion, politics, and education are profound and meaningful choices. Examine yourself, and you will discover everything in your life stems from choices. There are choices to be made every day. Become aware of these choices and the process you go through to come to a decision. Awareness is your greatest gift. Your awareness helps you understand the process of making decisions.

As you explore your choices, you begin to discover the amount of specifically detailed information you have about yourself. These facts lead you to your honest self. Your character needs to be just as detailed. These detailed choices bring truth to the moment. The truth is in the details.

Trust is important in making choices. Trust your instinct. Trust the material. Trust yourself. Awareness of your perspective and truth is important in making character choices. Your choices will be different from another actor's. Making a choice is risky business. It requires trust in yourself. Trust brings commitment to your choice. Live dangerously. Take the risk. These choices bring excitement and danger to your character. Doubt your choice only after you have fulfilled it and find it doesn't work. If you are living in your character's soul, you cannot view your work at the same time.

Everyone's experience leads her to different perceptions. Each person's perception is her personal and specific truth and honesty. This universal truth is shown in the play *Rashomon*. Three people have the same experience and perceive it three different ways. The deeper you commit to your instinct, the more personal, unique, and universal your character will be. You bring unique choices to your character's life. Trust yourself. Believe in your perceptions. Your choices allow the character to speak solely with your unique and original voice.

Make choices from the perspective of love. Choices should be positive. This gives you the widest range from which to choose. Negative choices, or choices from hate, lead you up a narrow and blind alley. This avenue offers a limited range of choices. Othello kills Desdemona out of love. He is so consumed with love for her he loses himself in the moment. He cannot bear the thought of anyone else being with her. If you play a killer, choose to support someone you care about. If the don of the Mafia asks you to kill someone for him, you do it for the love you have for him. He has taken care of your family. He has provided you with a good life. You have no feelings about the person you are going to kill. Your motivation for the murder is love of your benefactor. Take a moment, and observe the more varied range of choices you have when coming from the perspective of love.

Observe which images you allow to come into your consciousness. You choose what you wish to focus on. You see many images, but you focus only on specifically chosen ones. Images that please, satisfy, interest, intrigue, or even repel you. You eliminate many and come down to two or three. You take a moment. Scan the images. Settle on one. A choice.

You need to build a repertoire of varied characters and monologues: classical, contemporary, dramatic, comic, and even some monologues you just can't resist. Your classical choice need not be limited to Shakespeare. Moliere, Congreve, Sheridan, Euripedes, and Aeschylus wrote in verse and offer a wide range of multifaceted characters.

Singers have repertoires of songs ready to be performed at a moment's notice. The songs come from different periods and offer a variety of sounds, rhythms, and emotional content to showcase the singer's musical and interpretive talents. They have been learned both musically and lyrically. They have been interpreted and rehearsed and are ready to be sung whenever the right occasion arrives.

Choose monologues to show different aspects of your range and colors in your palette. Singers have up-tempo songs, ballads, show tunes, and torch songs. Actors create comic, tragic, evil, and good characters. Your choices express your aesthetic, taste, and interest. You reveal yourself through your choices.

There are situations when you are asked to perform a monologue or two contrasting monologues in three to five minutes; this is the standard amount of time to perform the miracle your audience wants to experience. Take your time and do the research. Choose wisely, and these three to five minutes can prove memorable. It is not how much time you have, but how well you use the time. Realizing your character and fulfilling the monologue in a short time is more effective than having lots of time and little impact. *Less is more.* Believe this. It's true.

Monologues fill many needs. They are used to put you on tape to be viewed on another coast or country for a film role or a commercial. Casting directors often have general calls to meet actors and see their work. From these viewings, they compile lists of actors to introduce to directors and artistic directors for different projects.

At regional theatres across the country, artistic directors produce a varied season by selecting plays by writers ranging from William Shakespeare to Wendy Wasserstein, involving styles as diverse as Greek tragedy or drawing room comedy. They need actors of range for their challenging seasons, actors at ease with language and behavior from different periods.

Costumes alone do not create the period. Wearing contemporary clothes and transporting your audience back in time with only language, behavior, and a moment-to-moment relationship with another person is the power of illusion and believing. *Acting is believing.* Belief in the circumstance and situation and a natural ease for language are key factors. Allowing your audience to discover your character's needs creates a union offering a meaningful experience. Choosing correctly and following this road map communicates your unique contributions to successfully fulfilling your character's monologue.

Your instinct plays an important role in making the right choices. Your initial reading of the material will elicit a gut reaction. This reaction is instinctual and subjective, and involves your senses. Trust it. Your instinctual and sensory awareness guides you in choosing correctly. Your goal is to get your audience to care about your character. To root for him to reach his objective. These immediate and instinctual feelings are what you want to share with your audience.

Stay with your instinct and feelings in the search for the right monologue. Don't soften or blur your reactions by intellectualizing. Leave your brain and its objectivity out of this piece of the process. Objective questions can help focus and guide you in your choices: What is the purpose of the monologue? Will it add to my repertoire? Does this character show new and different facets to my work? Will it broaden the viewer's perspective of my range? The answers here give additional guidance in choosing.

Once you have found a few monologues you like, you can begin the elimination process. Read the text. Allow it to affect you. Become aware of your connections with the characters and their monologues. Are you immediately connecting emotionally? Morally? Politically? Universally? Is your response to the characters' truth empathetic? Explore these questions and your instinctual responses. The exploration often proves more fruitful than the answers themselves.

Now read the monologues aloud. The words are meant to be spoken. Experience the emotional content as it moves through your body. Are you connecting with the character's need? Are you instinctively responding to the necessary emotional investment? All monologues, dramatic and comic, need a strong emotional investment. Your investment creates an emotional involvement carrying the audience on your character's emotional journey.

A monologue needs an emotional journey. The character begins in one emotional place and moves to another. There must be a dramatic event supporting the emotional change. The character's need should be of life-and-death importance to emotionally sustain the monologue. Look for urgency in the character's need. Does an inner conflict, fight, or struggle create action that emotionally propels the character in one direction or another?

The character's need to make a decision creates an inner struggle moving your character moment by moment closer to her objective. Some characters struggle internally and decide not to move forward or change. The moments leading to the decision creates movement. The decision-making process propels the emotional activity. The decision not to change is as specific and definite a choice as one to change. Going right, left, or remaining in the same emotional place are all choices activating your character's inner life.

Two contrasting monologues are what is most often asked of you. Contrast is one of the strongest confusions in choosing monologues. Contrasting? Happy and sad? Tragic and comic?

Often, actors choose a comic and serious monologue showing their ability to play comedy and drama. This choice shows a variation of a character evoking laughter or tears. The situation or circumstance may be contrasting, but the needs of the character are the same.

Characters with diametrically opposite souls offer contrast. Machiavelli and Forrest Gump or Lady Macbeth and Pollyanna are contrasting pairings. Characters motivated by different needs and opposing struggles to reach their objectives create contrast. These characters have differences in their souls, values, morals, ethos, and behavior. Consider aspects of character and monologue content when contrast is a deciding factor.

A classical character does not offer contrast with a contemporary character merely by the use of language or style. An introverted character in 1789 uses the same colors and shadings in 2005 and will show the same emotionality. His outside is contrasting, but the emotional truth of the characters is the same.

All people are different. Each an original. Subtlety and nuance make the difference. Awaken to the subtleties you instinctually feel. Experience the character with your senses. The awareness affecting your senses creates your individual voice. Your personal perceptions are yours alone. They have been created by *your* DNA, genes, upbringing, education, and observations, and bring you to your sense of aesthetics and values, both morally and politically. They combine to create your unique insight and perspective.

Explore these subtleties. Observe the nuances the monologue evokes in you. Each person is affected differently. Trust your own feelings. They are your truth. Become aware of the effect. Awareness aids in discovering your character. These effects create your palette of emotional colors and shadings. Committing your personal observations to your work creates an original, innovative, and complex character.

Likewise, characters are all different, as varied and specific as people. The deeper your commitment to your personal interpretation, the more successful you will be in capturing the audience's compassion, empathy, and support. Belief in your choices is paramount to bring commitment to the character while displaying your individual insights.

Trusting your instinct creates originality. Being original takes courage. Enjoy it. It offers others your specific and unique voice. Carbon copies lack specificity. Come through the door with your own personally insightful characterization, and watch your audience sit up and pay attention. There is always a demand for a new and original voice. Complex, interesting, surprising, and dangerous are qualities that excite. This excitement begins once you choose your monologues and begin the work toward an insightful and compelling interpretation.

The four monologues you will explore and fulfill here are contrasting. They illustrate how to apply the principles of the road map to all your work with monologues, songs, and monodramas. Edmund from *King Lear* by William Shakespeare, Serafina from *The Rose Tattoo* by Tennessee Williams. Beneatha from *A Raisin in the Sun* by Lorraine Hansberry, and Peter from *The Heidi Chronicles* by Wendy Wasserstein are diverse and contrasting people. They offer a cross section of humanity and literature.

Developing the four characters demonstrates the breadth of use of the road map. Creating a three-dimensional character alive in the moment allows the monologue to flow organically. Using the actor's tools helps realize your character. Adding the character's needs fulfills the monologue.

A familiar monologue is included to demonstrate how an original and insightful interpretation can transform familiarity into new life. A personal imprint on a monologue reveals your understanding of human behavior and involves your audience in a contemporary and fresh interpretation of the character. Don't shy away from a monologue because "it's done too often." Bring it to life with your personal insights and your interpretation makes it brand new.

William Shakespeare, Tennessee Williams, Lorraine Hansberry, and Wendy Wasserstein encompass a wide range of characters, all complex human beings living within complicated situations and circumstances. Different, yet humanly and emotionally similar. The differences separate. The humanity unites.

The authors offer a variety of writing styles. Each has a unique perception of humanity. They cover England, Louisiana, and middle America. They create four people living at different times and places. Fulfilling these four characters and their monologues by using the road map demonstrates the variety of roads there are to a compelling performance.

Choosing the monologue begins your road map to creating your character and her or his compelling monologue.

King Lear

by William Shakespeare

EDMUND:

> *Thou, Nature, art my goddess; to thy law*
> *My services are bound. Wherefore should I*
> *Stand in the plague of custom, and permit*
> *The curiosity of nations to deprive me,*
> *For that I am some twelve or fourteen moonshines*
> *Lag of a brother? Why bastard? Wherefore base,*
> *When my dimensions are as well compact,*
> *My mind as generous, and my shape as true,*
> *As honest madam's issue? Why brand they us*
> *With base? with baseness? bastardy? base, base?*
> *Who, in the lusty stealth of nature, take*
> *More composition and fierce quality*
> *Than doth, within a dull, stale, tired bed,*
> *Go to th' creating a whole tribe of fops*
> *Got 'tween asleep and wake? Well then,*
> *Legitimate Edgar, I must have your land.*
> *Our father's love is to the bastard Edmund*
> *As to th' legitimate. Fine word, "legitimate."*
> *Well, my legitimate, if this letter speed*
> *And my invention thrive, Edmund the base*
> *Shall top th' legitimate. I grow, I prosper.*
> *Now, gods, stand up for bastards!*

The Rose Tattoo

by Tennessee Williams

SERAFINA DELLE ROSE:

My folks was peasants, contadini, but he—he come from land-*owners!* Signorille, *my husband!—At night I sit here and I'm satisfied to remember, because I had the best.—Not the third best and not the second best, but the* first *best, the* only *best!—So now I stay here and am satisfied now to remember, ...I count up the nights I held him all night in my arms, and I can tell you how many. Each night for twelve years. Four thousand—three hundred—and eighty. The number of nights I held him all night in my arms. Sometimes I didn't sleep, just held him all night in my arms. And I am satisfied with it. I grieve for him. Yes, my pillow at night's never dry—but I'm satisfied to remember. And I would feel cheap and degraded and not fit to live with my daughter or under the roof with the urn of his blessed ashes, those—ashes of a rose—if after that memory, after knowing that man, I went to some other, some middle-aged man, not young, not full of young passion, but getting a pot belly on him and losing his hair and smelling of sweat and liquor—and trying to fool myself that* that *was love-making! I* know *what love-making was. And I'm satisfied just to remember ... Go on, you do it, you go on the streets and let them drop their sacks of dirty water on you!—I'm satisfied to remember the love of a man that was mine—only* mine! *Never touched by the hand of* nobody! Nobody *but* me!—Just me! Never nobody but me!*

A Raisin in the Sun

by Lorraine Hansberry

BENEATHA YOUNGER:

Me? ... Me? ... Me, I'm nothing ... Me. When I was very small ... we used to take our sleds out in the wintertime and the only hills we had were the ice-covered stone steps of some houses down the street. And we used to fill them in with snow and make them smooth and slide down them all day ... and it was very dangerous, you know ... far too steep ... and sure enough one day a kid named Rufus came down too fast and hit the sidewalk and we saw his face just split open right there in front of us ... And I remember standing there look-ing at his bloody open face thinking that was the end of Rufus. But the ambulance came and they took him to the hospital and they fixed the broken bones and they sewed it all up ... and the next time I saw Rufus he just had a little line down the middle of his face ... I never got over that ... That that was what one person could do for another, fix him up—sew up the problem, make him all right again. That was the most marvelous thing in the world ... I wanted to do that. I always thought it was the one concrete thing in the world that a human being could do. Fix up the sick, you know—and make them whole again. This was truly being God ... I wanted to cure. It used to be so important to me. I wanted to cure. It used to matter. I used to care. I mean about people and how their bodies hurt ... it doesn't seem deep enough, close enough to what ails mankind! It was a child's way of seeing things—or an idealist's.

The Heidi Chronicles

by Wendy Wasserstein

PETER PATRONE:

What a perky Seventies kind of gal you are! You can separate sexual needs from emotional dependencies. Heidi, if you tell me you secrete endorphins when you run, I'm going straight into the curator's office and demand an all armor retrospective.

Actually, I'm afraid I'm feeling sort of distant from you. I'm not criticizing you. It's just how I'm feeling. I haven't seen you in eight months.

Heidi, I don't play on your team. I've become a liberal homosexual pediatrician. And I prefer Stanley. My friend's name is Stanley Zinc. He's a child psychiatrist from Johns Hopkins. But he's thinking of quitting in order to study with Merce Cunningham. The sad thing is that Stanley is too old to join the company and Miss Merce isn't getting any younger, either. Anyway, I'm thinking of replacing him with a waiter I met last week, we share a mutual distrust of Laura Nyro. I would have told you all this earlier but I thought we deserved something more intimate than a phone call. So I chose the Chicago Art Institute.

Heidi, I'm gay, okay? I sleep with Stanley Zinc, M.D. And my *liberation,* my *pursuit of happiness,* and *the pursuit of happiness of other men like me is just as politically and socially valid as hanging a couple of Goddamned paintings because they were signed by someone named Nancy, Gladys, or Gilda. And that is why I came to see you today. I am demanding your equal time and consideration.*

2

Plumbing Your Text

You've chosen your monologue. Now what? Read the text. Whether it is a play, film script, novel, nonfiction work, or any other piece of writing, read the text from beginning to end. The text is your bible. It informs of your character's life, universe, relationships, circumstances and situation. Details about your character begin to be revealed as you read. Most of the information you need is within these pages. Careful scrutiny will answer most of your questions. Begin visualizing your character's existence. Discover the facts of her or his life. Each fact is a clue. Each clue is a dot in connecting the dots to realize your character.

Think back to when you played connect the dots as a child. You began at dot number one, and when you arrived at the last dot, you had a face. If you missed any of the dots, your face might have only one ear or a flattened head. Find all the clues to create a complete and clear character for your audience.

Plumbing the text yields information about your character and your character's life, relationships with others, and behavioral patterns. It may not be clearly laid out, but there are clues imbedded in the text. These clues bring specificity to the character. They lead to your character's actions and behavior. What she says and how she interacts with other characters offers insight. What others say about your character may not always be the truth. Look for clues as a detective does. The clues come in different forms, both obvious and subtle. The clues aid in carefully and specifically connecting the dots. All information helps in building your character and interpreting her monologue.

Now read the text again. Only this time subjectively, from your character's perspective. Experience the universe your character inhabits through his eyes, ears, and being. Involve your instinct. Trust it to guide you. This is the first step in turning yourself over to your character. Important aspects of your character's emotional truth and psychological makeup can be discovered by allowing the sensory elements to affect you. Embrace your character's feelings about his surroundings. Learn how he is affected by the climate, season, and time of day and how he feels about his particular situation and circumstance. Gather facts about your character's life. Facts are tangible; they ground your character in reality. Allow your senses and the facts to take you inside your character.

Your character's behavior is subjective, and switching to the "I" viewpoint allows you an immediate and informative connection. Read from the "I" perspective. "I" am the character. See, hear, taste, touch, and smell everything as you familiarize yourself with the text and gain intimacy with your character.

The clues reveal the depth of the character's joy, pain, passion, desire, and need. Characters, like people, are ambivalent. Don't overlook these ambiguities. "No, no, no" can mean "yes, yes, yes," or even "maybe, maybe, maybe." The ambiguities bring interest and complexity to your character. These complexities enrich your character by creating surprise and mystery. Clues reveal patterns of behavior imprinted by events in your character's life, helping you understand your character and her needs. Question and explore anything that makes a light bulb go on in your head. Don't overlook anything that jolts you during the exploration process.

Begin to create your character's world in the present. Her circumstance and situation are her here and now. The circumstances are the facts of her life, the building blocks for her foundation. Believe in her circumstances totally. These are the given truths. Make them specific, real, and personal to you. This is where the commitment begins.

The situation happens in the present, making the character's emotional life alive and urgent. Accept his situation as your own. This acceptance allows you to be affected by the obstacles and pressures your character experiences in the moment. This acceptance begins creating the world of your character.

You may discover important and helpful facts or clues, along with seemingly unimportant ones, showing the effect of events and actions on your character's life, needs, and motivations. The perception of these effects and their impacted results add specificity to your interpretation. Small or large imprints on his life inform and shade moments. These imprints help justify your character's behavior. The information leads you to your character's objective. The objective is the spine of your character. It creates his emotional journey moving him forward, action by action and dot by dot.

Now, subjectively view each of the four characters and their stories. See how their universes revolve around them, making each the center of their universe.

Edmund—from *King Lear* by William Shakespeare

Identifying Edmund's Story

Having just returned from nine years away at school, Edmund is introduced to the Earl of Kent by his father, the Earl of Gloucester, as his younger and illegitimate son whose presence causes him great embarrassment. Edmund hears he will soon be sent away again.

The news of his imminent exile propels Edmund to take immediate action to win his father's love and approval. He calls upon Nature, his goddess, for help in gaining a rightful place in his father's and society's eyes. He also feels deserving of his share of his father's estate, all of which his legitimate and older brother, Edgar, stands to inherit.

Obsessively, Edmund puts his plan into action. To discredit Edgar, he forges a letter detailing a plot to kill their father. He then withholds the letter from Gloucester, manipulating him into demanding it. Gloucester questions Edmund's knowledge of

Edgar's plan. At Gloucester's insistence, Edmund affirms it is Edgar's handwriting.

Edgar's arrival prompts Edmund to seize the opportunity. He tells Edgar Gloucester is at war with him and suggests Edgar hide in his, Edmund's, house. He convinces Edgar to arm himself with a sword against their father. Edmund delights in having created a mutual distrust between his father and brother. His plan is in motion.

Curan, Gloucester's servant, arrives and tells Edmund that Cornwall and Regan are on their way. Trouble is brewing between the Dukes of Cornwall and Albany, husbands to Regan and Goneril, respectively. He decides to aid Cornwall to heighten the threat against Edgar.

Edmund rouses Edgar from his hiding place and informs him of Cornwall's anger toward him for siding with Albany. He also tells Edgar their father has discovered his hiding place. Hearing Gloucester approach, he insists Edgar draw his sword against him and then forces Edgar to flee. He cuts himself on his arm and tells Gloucester that Edgar cut him for refusing to take part in his plot to kill their father. Gloucester praises Edmund as a loyal and natural boy. Edmund is succeeding in gaining his father's recognition and acceptance as a legitimate son and heir.

Cornwall and Regan arrive. Gloucester and Edmund affirm Edgar's participation with some "riotous" knights against Regan's father, King Lear, and tells of his actions against Gloucester.

Gloucester calls upon Edmund to distract Cornwall while he goes in search of Lear. He informs Edmund if Cornwall notices his absence he will be tried for treason. Edmund seizes this opportunity. He immediately tells Cornwall of Gloucester's search for Lear and about a letter describing the French invasion. Edmund hopes his complicity with the newly anointed royal couple will get them to bestow his father's title, land, and fortune upon him.

Edmund, hoping to become King of England, convinces both Goneril and Regan of his love for each. Setting each against the other for his affections, they become enemies.

Cornwall bestows Gloucester's title upon Edmund, pronouncing him the Earl of Gloucester, and asks him to accompany Goneril and bring Albany Gloucester's traitorous letter. Hearing of Albany's displeasure with Regan's treatment of Lear, Goneril immediately directs Edmund to go to Cornwall and raise the troops against the French, telling him she will take the power from Albany. She kisses Edmund farewell with a more than friendly kiss.

Edmund arrives to find Cornwall dead so he himself leads the British army against France. Regan, now a widow, demands to know where Edmund's affections lie. He convinces Regan he has no feeling for Goneril and has never been intimate with her.

Albany joins Edmund's army against the French invasion. Edgar, disguised as a messenger, shows Edmund Goneril's letter asking him to kill Albany. Edmund returns with news of the advancement of the French. Albany hurries out.

With the sisters warring against each other for his affection, Edmund stands to inherit all of Lear's land and become King of England.

Having captured Cordelia and Lear, Edmund sends them away and gives instructions for their death. Albany, arriving with Regan and Goneril, praises Edmund's bravery. He demands to know where Cordelia and Lear are. Edmund lies, telling Albany they have been sent away to prevent them from gaining sympathy and causing an insurgence. Albany rebukes him for placing himself above his place, but Regain intervenes. She says she will marry Edmund and make him King, giving him total charge. Goneril says Edmund will never marry Regan.

Albany intervenes and arrests Edmund on charges of treason. Challenging Edmund to defend himself in a duel, Albany brings on a masked champion who wounds Edmund. The masked champion is Edgar. Albany asks Edgar to spare Edmund's life so they may learn the whereabouts of Cordelia and Lear.

As Edmund lies dying, a messenger rushes in to inform everyone that Goneril has fatally stabbed herself and poisoned Regan. Edmund repents, and wishing to redeem himself, he admits ordering the hanging of Cordelia. He immediately sends a messenger to stop the act before it is too late.

As he dies, Edmund realizes, and announces, that he has indeed been loved.

Defining Edmund's Circumstance

It is the eighth century BC, a barbaric and often savage period inhabited by people behaving brutally. Edmund is the illegitimate son of the Earl of Gloucester and thus banned from receiving or sharing in his father's estate. He has returned from nine years away at school and has just learned he will be sent away again immediately.

Focusing Edmund's Situation

In the opening moments of the play, Edmund is introduced to the Earl of Kent by his father, the Earl of Gloucester. Gloucester's first words tell of Edmund's illegitimate birth and express his embarrassment at Edmund's very presence.

> *I have so often blushed to acknowledge him.*

It is like a bell unceasingly bonging in his ears. BASTARD!!! BASE!!! It is as alive as an unrelieved headache or toothache. He has lived with this truth all of his life, making him feel unloved, less than his brother Edgar, and a second-class citizen to all around him.

Gloucester's insensitivity reawakens the emotional pain Edmund has kept under control for the nine years he has been away at school. He is on fire with rage.

The very next moment, Gloucester expresses love for Edmund.

> *But I have a son, sir, by order of law, some year*
> *elder than this who yet is no dearer in my account*
> *. . .*

This Edmund cannot hear.

Gloucester follows this with the news Edmund will be sent away again, causing Edmund to realize his mere presence represents Gloucester's very public infidelity. Edmund now knows he must take immediate action to gain his father's approval and respect. He views Edgar, his brother, as his true rival.

Analyzing Edmund

Edmund is a young man with a dark and troubled soul seeking love and approval. Defined by his father's adulterous indiscretion, he is referred to as Edmund the illegitimate, Edmund the bastard, or Edmund the base. He has been exiled at school for the last nine years, living among strangers without love, warmth, or nurturing during his formative years. Edmund's profound need for his father's love and acceptance drive him to seek his rightful place. This abusive treatment at his father's hands has created jealousy and distrust toward his brother Edgar, who is loved by Gloucester and stands to inherit their father's entire estate.

Never having experienced warmth and tenderness, Edmund believes he has to manipulate for love. He is obsessed with the need to be accepted and respected by the society he lives in. Feeling looked down on, he needs to convince himself he is worthy. By manipulating Goneril and Regan into loving him, he believes he will be made King of England and force all to love, respect, and accept him.

Edmund is cunning and strong. He is a product of isolation, emotional abuse and the brutal savagery of his time. He is a wounded soul.

Investigating Clues to Edmund's Truth

Immediately following the news he will be sent away again by his embarrassed father, Edmund delivers his emotional monologue, fueled by his need for love and approval multiplied by the urgency of his impending banishment.

Gloucester's ambivalence and abusive feelings deeply disturb and confuse Edmund. One moment Gloucester ridicules him, the next he says he cares for him. Then he immediately says Edmund will be sent away again. What is the truth? What can Edmund believe? Love and hurt comingle in Edmund's world.

Edgar, his older brother, is held in high esteem by his father. He is King Lear's godson, the godson of the King of England. It is a truth Edmund can never change.

Edmund calls on a higher being, Nature, to guide him. What is Nature to him? Is it God? Is it a higher universal power? He believes in Nature's fairness to the legitimate and illegitimate.

Edmund's insecurity drives him to believe his only option is to dispose of his competition for his father's love. These are not the needs of a villain. These are the needs of an abused and unloved human being searching for parental love and acceptance. This is a universally recognizable emotional truth.

Being illegitimate in the eighth century offers little chance of gaining a good woman's hand in marriage. No father will want his daughter to marry him. What does the future hold for him?

The belief in Nature running through the play highlights the importance of belief. Mutual distrust amongst most of the characters informs of the harshness of the time. Lying appears to be everyone's modus operandi. The truth is a mystery. Edmund needs to emotionally isolate and protect himself.

Pinpointing the Dramatic Event

Gloucester's announcement of Edmund's being sent away raises the stakes and creates a greater importance and urgency, forcing Edmund into immediate action. He must end his father's ridicule and the pain it causes him.

Gloucester's seemingly tossed-off announcement to send Edmund away is of mammoth import to Edmund's life and propels him to take actions affecting everyone. The impact of this news drives Edmund throughout the play.

Arriving at Decisions

Convincing himself of Nature's approval, Edmund decides to fight for his right to be accepted as a legitimate son and heir by putting his plan into action.

Serafina delle Rose—from *The Rose Tattoo* by Tennessee Williams

Identifying Serafina's Story

Serafina delle Rose, nicely dressed, sits in front of a prettily set dining table awaiting the arrival of her husband, Rosario. Rosario, who has saved enough to begin his own business, is returning from his last delivery of banana-concealed contraband. As each truck goes by, Serafina waits with bated breath for it to stop and bring home the man she so loves. Their twelve-year-old daughter, Rosa, is playing in front of the house.

Serafina lives for Rosario. She was a fourteen-year-old peasant girl in Sicily when she married Rosario, whose family were landowners. He brought her to this devoutly Catholic Sicilian community on Louisiana's Gulf Coast. Their marriage, she feels, raised her status, so she believes she owes everything to Rosario. She is the community seamstress, bringing in extra money.

Assunta, a neighbor, comes in to sell her powders and potions that enhance sexual performance. Serafina brags Rosario is a perfect lover and that she is pregnant. At the moment of conception, she felt a pain in her chest and awoke to find Rosario's rose tattoo transplanted onto her breast.

Estelle Hohengarten arrives asking Serafina to make a shirt for the man she loves. She has brought rose-colored silk and offers to pay anything to have the shirt ready the next day.

Early the next morning Serafina is awakened by the voices of her priest and neighbors and learns immediately Rosario has been killed when his truck exploded. She collapses.

Later that day, Serafina learns she has lost her baby. In an act of defiance against the Catholic church, Serafina demands that Rosario be cremated and his ashes kept in an urn on her altar alongside the statue of Our Lady.

Three years later, Serafina, still in mourning, has allowed herself to become disheveled and overweight. It is Rosa's high school graduation day.

For dancing with a boy at a school dance, Rosa has been confined to the house and not permitted to go to school. Miss Yorke, her teacher, arrives to demand Rosa be allowed to attend her graduation.

Serafina tells the teacher the school is ruining her daughter by allowing her to meet boys at the young age of fifteen. In Sicily, young girls do not dance with boys they are not engaged to. Serafina repents and agrees to let Rosa attend her graduation.

As Serafina is getting ready to go to the graduation, Flora and Bessie, two local women, come to pick up a blouse Serafina has been paid to make for Flora. The blouse is not finished, and Serafina is in a rush to get to Rosa's graduation. Flora threatens to expose her for working without a license. Serafina's sewing is now the sole income she and Rosa have to live on. She agrees to finish the blouse.

Serafina sews and listens as the women discuss their prurient reasons for going to New Orleans. She tells them of love and the purity of a relationship. They taunt her with news of Rosario's affair with Estelle Hohengarten. It seems everyone knew of the affair except Serafina. Serafina calls them liars, screams and chases them from the house. Realizing the woman who wanted the rose-colored silk shirt is Estelle, she denies Rosario was having an affair and begs Our Lady to give her a sign of the truth. Music from the high school band alerts her the graduation is beginning. She is paralyzed with fury and cannot move.

Serafina has closed all the shutters locking out the world. She sits in total darkness as Rosa and her boyfriend Jack arrive. Rosa needs to change clothes and join her classmates for a picnic. Seeing the darkened, locked house, Rosa assumes Serafina is out. Inside, Rosa calls Jack to her and begins an intimate conversation. Serafina, wearing a slip, surprises them. Rosa sees Serafina's physical and emotionally numb state. Serafina refuses to tell her what happened. Trying to dress Serafina quickly to introduce her to Jack, Rosa tries to lighten the mood by showing her mother her diploma and the award she won. Serafina is numb and immovable. She is paralyzed by having heard Rosa trying to seduce Jack. She believes Jack will be Rosa's ruination.

Rosa leaves to change her clothes, and Serafina rouses herself. She gets Jack to admit they have not been intimate and that he is both a virgin and Catholic. She demands he kneel to Our Lady and swear he will not lay a hand on Rosa. He complies, and Serafina gives her okay for them to go on the picnic. Rosa is ecstatic and asks her mother to open a bottle of wine in celebration. As Serafina uncorks the wine, Rosa's friends arrive. She and Jack run off. As they get into the car, Serafina remembers the Bulova watch she bought as a graduation present. Alone, Serafina once again asks Our Lady for a sign of truth about Rosario.

Later that day, Father De Leo, Serafina's priest, arrives to try to get her out of her lethargy. Serafina demands to know if Rosario told him of an affair with Estelle Hohengarten. He refuses to break the laws of the church. He cannot reveal what has been told in the confessional. She goes wild, beginning to howl and scream like an animal. She attacks Father De Leo. As he runs out, Serafina collapses on the steps.

Alvaro Mangiacavallo comes along, following a salesman whose car is preventing Alvaro from moving his banana-filled truck. Following a screaming fight, Alvaro goes into the house and begins to cry, as he admits he usually does after a fight. He is embarrassed and doesn't want anyone to see him. Serafina agrees to sew his torn jacket. As he removes it, Serafina sees the body of Rosario on Alvaro.

She takes this as the sign she has been waiting for. He is Sicilian. He hauls bananas. He has the body of Rosario. She knows this is what Our Lady has planned for her. She gets a bottle of wine to celebrate. She tells him of Rosario, his rose tattoo, and the saving of his ashes. Alvaro assures her a body can decay but ashes always stay clean. She offers him the rose-colored silk shirt she made for Estelle. He feels it is too good for him, but she insists. They share experiences of their lives and seems to have a lot in common.

Serafina tells him to come back later that evening for his jacket but only if the lights are on in the house. She explains about Rosa, saying it would not be good if she is home. He agrees.

Later that night Alvaro sees the house lit up and comes in. He is all cleaned up and has oil of rose in his hair. Serafina is also cleaned up, and Alvaro is struck by her appearance. She gets some wine. He tells her he has had a rose tattooed on his chest. She is struck by this but uncertain of her feelings. He wants to get romantic. She is reticent about moving too quickly.

Serafina asks Alvaro to take her to the Square Roof, a casino where Estelle is a black jack dealer. She wants to cut out Estelle's tongue. Alvaro tells her he knows Estelle and assures Serafina Estelle would not have done such a thing. On the phone with Serafina listening, Estelle admits to the affair and expresses her love for Rosario. Serafina goes wild. Alvaro calms her down.

Serafina feels the need for propriety. She asks Alvaro to play along with a masquerade. She tells him to leave and return unseen. They loudly say goodnight. He leaves. She darkens the house. He reenters through the back door. They drink wine and retire to the bedroom.

The next morning, with Rosa asleep on the sofa in her slip, Serafina asks Alvaro to leave. Rosa awakens, and Serafina tries to hide the truth from her. They argue. Rosa runs out. Again, Serafina misses her opportunity to give Rosa the Bulova watch.

As the neighbors gather in the yard, Serafina runs off to be with Alvaro.

Defining Serafina's Circumstance

Serafina and her daughter, Rosa, live in a devoutly Catholic, heavily Sicilian village on Louisiana's Gulf Coast in 1950. It is a hot and humid environment. Still in mourning three years after her husband, Rosario, was killed, Serafina has built a protective wall of denial about Rosario's infidelity and refuses to move on with her life.

Choosing to remain in the past and using Rosario's ashes to keep their love alive, she is in a profound state of depression, unkempt and disheveled. Flora and Bessie arrive to collect the unfinished blouse Flora paid Serafina to make.

Focusing Serafina's Situation

It is Rosa's graduation day, and Serafina, trying to dress, is interrupted by Flora and Bessie. Threatened with exposure for working without a license, Serafina agrees to finish the blouse.

Incensed by their tawdriness, Serafina, ever the good Catholic, shares the depth and beauty of the love she shared with Rosario. They retaliate with news of Rosario's affair with Estelle Hohengarten. She rushes them out of the house and prays to Our Lady for the truth.

Analyzing Serafina

Serafina delle Rose is a devout Catholic. Yet she defies the church by demanding Rosario's cremation and so shows the enormity of her strength and determination. Her dedication to Rosario three years after his death is expressed by her deep depression.

Serafina is a dominant and powerful personality. She clutches to the love she shared with Rosario. She is fiercely protective of Rosa, wanting only the best for her, the best as an old world Sicilian woman knows it.

Serafina is a woman refusing to live in the present and determined to remain loyal to Rosario. She denies the truth about Rosario, needing to hear from God to believe it. She is a powerful romantic. She opts to live in the past when life was simpler and less complicated. She doesn't want Rosa to grow up. Subconsciously, she is yearning for someone to awaken her.

Investigating Clues to Serafina's Truth

Serafina is a good Sicilian wife living for her husband and a devout Catholic living by the tenets of the church. The altar in her living room shows the importance of the church in her life. Standing up to her priest, church, and the entire Catholic community displays her ferociousness. The strength and power of her determination is an indicator of the profundity of her denial.

Her love and protection of Rosa expresses her old world beliefs. Her disdain toward Flora and Bessie informs of her desire to keep the modern world from entering her home.

The amount of sewing work she gets tells us she is a good seamstress.

Serafina is a contradiction unto herself. Dominant and vulnerable. Believing in her religion and defying it at the same time.

By invading her world with the truth Flora and Bessie turn Serafina into a wild and untamed animal. Their words strengthen her determination to continue believing in her own truth about Rosario and to remain in the past.

Ambiguity abounds in Serafina as shown by her actions toward and against the church and in her dealings with Rosa, Jack, and Alvaro. She is unaware of her desire to be aroused from her lethargy. She displays a robust and abundant sense of humor.

Pinpointing the Dramatic Event

While sharing intimate details of her emotional and physical love with Rosario with Flora and Bessie, she rekindles her desire to love and be loved. This has awakened her feelings of emptiness, loss, and yearning.

Arriving at Decisions

Serafina reawakens to the depth of love she shared with Rosario. She affirms her desire to devote herself to him in death as she did in life, unconciously strengthening her denial.

Beneatha Younger—from *A Raisin in the Sun* by Lorraine Hansberry

Identifying Beneatha's Story

It is Friday morning, in the early 1950s on Chicago's South Side. Beneatha Younger comes out of the bedroom she shares with her mother, holding her toothbrush, toothpaste, and towel, ready to use the bathroom down the hall her family shares with their neighbors.

Her older brother, Walter Lee, sits at the kitchen table; his wife, Ruth, prepares breakfast; and their seven-year-old son, Travis, has left for school after making his bed, which is the family sofa.

Beneatha is in a rush, needing to get to her college class on time. She is studying to be a doctor and hopes to bring honor to the Younger family. She is proud of her dream. She is determined to rise above the expected paths taken by Negroes (the term African

American had not yet come into use) in this period. Her mother and sister-in-law work as domestics, her brother as a chauffeur.

Her morning begins with an argument with Walter Lee over insurance money the family is expecting from their father's recent death. Sibling rivalry and jealousy built on love is how she interacts with him. Beneatha professes to want none of the money. It belongs to their mother. Beneatha's family tries keeping her in reality. The reality of being a colored woman. She bucks them at every turn. Believing in self-expression, she has tried photography, acting, and horseback riding and is now beginning guitar lessons. She is serious about being a doctor.

She is dating George Murchison, a fellow student from a well-to-do family. Beneatha finds him shallow. George believes the doctor phase will pass and Beneatha will come to her senses. Her family wants her to marry George.

Her mother believes very strongly in God. Beneatha is irreverent, believing man's triumphs are due to science and man himself. She expresses her anti-God feelings in a forthright manner, angering her mother to the point of slapping Beneatha's face. The youngest in the family and a woman, Beneatha does not feel as free to express herself as Walter Lee. Feeling this constraint she colors her opinions with wit and sarcasm.

Beneatha's other beau, Asagai, is an exchange student from Nigeria. Asagai begins awakening Beneatha to her African heritage, giving her an authentic Nigerian robe and music. She has very warm feelings for Asagai. He respects her dreams.

Later that evening, decked out in full Nigerian attire, including headdress, she waits for George, who is taking her to the theatre. George arrives and asks her to change into something less showy. She feels stifled by George and his assimilationist ideas. She believes he wants to turn her into another colored woman with no dreams of her own. She acquiesces and obeys his wish.

Mama has made a down payment on a three-bedroom house. Beneatha is thrilled. The next day, Mr. Lindner, from the "Welcoming Committee" of the new neighborhood, offers to buy back the house from the colored family planning to move into his white neighborhood. Walter Lee turns down his offer, filling Beneatha with pride in him.

As the family revels in their joy, the doorbell rings. It is a friend of Walter Lee's, informing him that the money he invested in the liquor store has been stolen by their partner. All is lost, including the money Mama gave Walter Lee to put away for Beneatha's education.

An hour later Asagai drops in to help with the Younger's packing, Beneatha is numb and despairing from the loss of her future. Asagai explains life is not about money, especially other people's money. He asks her to come to Nigeria with him and practice medicine there.

Walter Lee calls Mr. Lindner to take up the neighborhood's offer to buy back the house at a profit. Beneatha feels contempt for her brother. He has robbed her of her future and their mother of her new home.

Mr. Lindner arrives. The family gathers. Walter Lee, prodded by Mama to show Travis the kind of man he is, says he is proud of Beneatha's ambition to become a doctor. Again he refuses the offer, saying the family will work together to pay for the house. Beneatha is proud and filled with love for Walter Lee. She sees a man she can respect emerge from the ashes.

Defining Beneatha's Circumstance

Beneatha lives with her family in a cramped two-bedroom apartment. They share a hall bathroom with their neighbors. She has no privacy. Her family invades her space.

Beneatha lives her life as a feminist. Ahead of her time, she breaks with her family's tradition of acceptance and assimilation, constantly defending against their resistance to her growth and dreams of becoming a doctor.

She is torn between two beaus, wealthy George Murchison, offering her a secure and assimilated middle class life, and Asagai, offering her a life in Nigeria steeped in her African roots and with a medical practice.

Focusing Beneatha's Situation

Walter Lee's loss of the money for her medical education leaves Beneatha emotionally empty and numb. Without her dreams, she feels she is nothing.

Analyzing Beneatha

More than a decade before the civil rights movement and two decades before the feminist movement, Beneatha at 20, attempts to practice equality in both arenas. An early voice for women and the emerging civil rights movement, she believes the American dream also applies to Negroes and women. She is studying medicine, planning to become a doctor. She independently creates a new and adventurous path in life while bucking her family's traditionalism. She is the first member of her family to go to college. Her drive to become a doctor displays her strength and determination. She is a trailblazer encountering resistance from everyone, except Asagai.

She is outspoken and constantly defends her independence with wry and acerbic humor. In defiance to her mother, she is irreverent about her feelings toward God.

She has a scientific nature and wants everything proven to her. She is intelligent and focused. She believes in the importance of integrity and morality. Beneatha is totally outspoken in all areas of her life: personally, religiously, professionally, culturally, socially, and politically.

Beneatha's two beaus and her relationship with each reveals much about her. With George, she is obedient. With Asagai, she is a dreamer and adventurer.

Investigating Clues to Beneatha's Truth

She reads the newspaper, expressing her interest and curiosity. This simple action sets her apart from her family. Her acerbic and witty outspokenness is belied by her actions that reveal a need to protect her vulnerability and idealism. Her words about God show her defiant nature and express her profound belief in science.

Her many contradictions remind us of her youthful rebellion. She expresses her feelings about George but responds to his wishes. She changes from her African garb when he asks her to. She talks against assimilation yet straightens her hair. There is also her short-lived self expression in photography, painting, dance, and acting.

When Ruth announces she is pregnant, Beneatha snidely asks if the new baby is going to sleep on the roof. She then recants and apologizes, expressing her love and her awareness of Ruth's feelings.

She tells Asagai she will not be his American episode, showing her feelings toward men.

Beneatha's intensity and self-importance are humorous. Her speech is sprinkled with Italian and French phrases that show both her education and her need to feel superior to her family.

Pinpointing the Dramatic Event

Walter Lee's actions have left Beneatha helpless to fulfill her dreams. She reexamines her reasons for wanting to become a doctor and reawakens her solid belief in doctors and the medical profession. She rekindles her lost dream.

Arriving at Decisions

Beneatha fights against her feelings of despair and nothingness. She discovers her dreams were based on more than a desire to achieve. She needs to care for humanity. She decides to move forward toward her dream.

Peter Patrone—from *The Heidi Chronicles* by Wendy Wasserstein

Identifying Peter's Story

At a senior high school dance in 1965, Peter meets Heidi. He flirts, using French expressions and musical and literary allusions. Heidi picks up the ball and responds in kind. Their lifelong friendship begins.

It is 1974, the day of Richard Nixon's resignation. Outside the Chicago Art Institute, Heidi is picketing for Women in Art. Peter, now an intern, arrives irate with Heidi, who had telephoned saying she had no time to see him. He feels emotionally shortchanged. Her ideology means more to her than their friendship.

He tells her he is gay, which does not make Heidi happy. He shares his relationship with Dr. Stanley Zinc. Ever the nurturing male, Peter is concerned that Heidi's interest in the movement is overshadowing her personal and emotional growth.

At a TV studio in New York City in 1982, Peter, Heidi and Scoop, Heidi's secret love, are being prepped for their appearance on "Hello New York." They represent the baby boom generation. Peter is now a pediatrician at New York Hospital.

On the air, Peter is prompted to exploit his homosexual lifestyle, bringing out his cynicism. He aggressively competes with Scoop and almost entirely shuts Heidi out of the interview. Peter is appalled at Scoop's pretensions.

It is midnight in 1987, Heidi appears at the children's ward of New York Hospital, where Peter heads the pediatric division, to donate boxes of her old belongings and informs Peter she is moving to Minnesota to begin life anew. Peter is furious at her lack of emotional involvement in life. He explains what the AIDS epidemic has done to his life and his friends, how important she is to him, and how she lacks depth in her personal relationships.

Peter's emotional pain is palpable. Finally managing to reach Heidi, she decides to stay, acknowledging the importance of their twenty-five year friendship.

Defining Peter's Circumstance

Peter is standing outside the Chicago Art Institute. He is angry at Heidi's unwillingness to find time to spend with him. A protest meeting is gathering as he tries to talk to her. People, noise, commotion, and Heidi's preoccupation force him to demand her attention.

Focusing Peter's Situation

Peter arrives to Heidi's news that she is no longer involved with Scoop but enjoys sleeping with him. Peter is horrified at Heidi's emotional compartmentalization and feels the need to get through her protective shell. He tells her that she can't take their relationship for granted. Peter feels the need to tell her about his homosexuality and his relationship.

Analyzing Peter

Peter Patrone is an upper middle class, gay, Italian-American pediatrician in his late twenties. As a graduate of Williams College, a well-respected liberal arts college, he is musically and literarily knowledgeable. He savors his well-rounded education. His conversation is sprinkled with French phrases, musical and literary references. He is articulate, well informed, and active, both socially and politically. He has a playful and fantasy-filled romantic nature along with a sharp-tongued sense of humor.

Peter's feelings for Heidi deepen over the years. His jealousy of Scoop strengthens over the course of the play. Peter is accepting of his homosexuality except where Heidi is involved. He lives with pained feelings that his orientation does not allow him to share a life with her.

Peter has a nurturing nature, shown by his concern for Heidi and his choice of pediatrics. As a gay man, he will probably not have any children of his own. Pediatrics allows him to nurture and have children in his life.

Peter is a complex late twentieth-century, sophisticated, well-educated, urban gay man trying to make life simple for himself. His monologue shows humor, bitterness, aggression, love, intelligence, fear, and truth.

Investigating Clues to Peter's Truth

Peter's use of literary and musical references shows their importance for him. When he first meets Heidi, he calls himself a small noise from Winnetka, a reference to Gene Krupa's hit song "Big Noise from Winnetka." By calling himself a "small" noise, he reveals his feelings about himself.

In his monologue, he mentions Laura Nyro, a songwriter of highly political and deeply-felt emotional songs, expressing a sensitive nature that he is always trying to hide.

When he first meets Heidi, Peter searches to guess her name choosing names of three well-known literary characters, Amanda from *Private Lives* by Noel Coward, Lady Clara from *Castle Richmond* by Anthony Trollope, and Estelle from *Great Expectations* by Charles Dickens. These references, along with the sanitarium scenario from *The Magic Mountain* by Thomas Mann, reveal the breadth of reading he has already done in his young life. These references and his college choice inform us of the importance literature and knowledge plays and will play in Peter's life.

He is both a liberal and homosexual, and uncomfortable with the hip guys. He introduces himself to Heidi after seeing her shield her friend Susan. Seeming uncomfortable and displaying concern for Susan, Heidi appears to Peter to be his kindred spirit.

Plumbing the text gives an insightful picture of the complex relationship Peter has with Scoop, his competitor for Heidi's love. Scoop, the liberal intellectual, is ever present in Peter's existence when he is with Heidi. Peter's homosexuality prevents him from having sex with Heidi and adds to his negative feelings toward Scoop. In Peter's perception, Scoop treats her shabbily and Heidi's need allows her to accept Scoop's callowness.

His own relationship with Stanley lasts throughout most of his adult life, despite trials, tribulations, and temptation from other men. It is important to track the course of their relationship.

Peter wears jeans, defining him as a casual person who is not uptight. He carries a backpack and an umbrella, informing us he is always prepared. He is aware of the world and his own personal needs.

This play, unlike the other three, jumps in time. It is important to know specifically what happens to Peter in the intervening years. How does he change from decade to decade? How does the appearance of AIDS and HIV affect his life?

Pinpointing the Dramatic Event

Peter struggles with his conflict about and love for Heidi, forcing him to reveal himself and forever change their relationship.

Arriving at Decisions

Peter decides to tell Heidi of his lifestyle and relationship with Stanley Zinc to help Heidi wake up to her emotionally empty life.

3

Interpreting the Monologue Subjectively

You have chosen a monologue, plumbed the text for your character's story, defined the circumstances, focused the situation, analyzed your character, investigated for clues looking for their truth, pinpointed the dramatic event that moves them forward, and arrived at decisions they need to make. All of this work has been objective and used your intellect.

Now you are ready to begin interpreting the monologue from the character's perspective. This is the start of your subjective work. It requires you to forego using your intellect and come from an emotional and sensory place. Each character experiences their situation and circumstances internally. Their perspective may differ from the objective truth, but it is how they perceive it and for them it is the truth. Their truth.

Edmund

Edmund calls on Nature to help him proceed with a plan to gain his father's love and acceptance. At the same time, he informs her of his loyalty.

> *Thou, Nature, art my goddess; to thy law*
> *My services are bound.*

He shares the trivial reasons for his being scorned. They are mere technicalities. Being the second born is irrelevant. He describes himself as good looking, as smart, and as deserving as Edgar. Therefore, why is he branded with being base, a bastard, illegitimate? It was Gloucester, Edmund's father who strayed from his marital bed. Is he to be punished for his father's sins?

The inequity he feels can only be corrected by disgracing Edgar in their father's eyes. He feels his strength grow as he experiences Nature affirming his thoughts and understanding his need for acceptance.

The last straw comes with:

> *Our father's love is to the bastard Edmund*
> *As to the legitimate.*

The realization and acceptance of:

> *Fine word, "legitimate"!*

With these three words, Edmund realizes he can never rectify this circumstance, and only action will grant him his rightful place. Even with this revelation, he is not convinced.

> *Well, my legitimate, if this letter speed*
> *And my invention thrive, Edmund the base*
> *Shall top the legitimate.*

He doesn't say this letter will speed. He says "*if*." This two-letter word is very important. He has still not reached his decision. He ponders what may happen if he gets this letter into his father's hands, but at this moment, he is not yet convinced it is the right choice.

Does Nature actually give him the green light for his plan? Or does he convince himself he needs to put his plan into action?

> *I grow, I prosper . . . .*

This rallying cry and his personal need to grow and prosper close him off to Nature's guidance. In the moment he is unable to see, hear, or feel anything other than his needs.

Now, gods, stand up for bastards!

Defiantly he tells the gods what to do. Did Nature affirm or grant his objective? It appears he is convinced Nature has given him her approval.

Moment-to-moment reality is very important. Don't allow Edmund to get ahead of himself.

Edmund's actions and the effect of his actions depict his desperate need to be loved and accepted. Would a universal power of good lead him to the bloodshed his action causes? Would he be led to his untimely death?

His monologue shows intelligence, reverence, humor, defensiveness, common sense, jealousy, desire for his father's love, and a profound need to cover the rejection he lives with every moment of his life.

Serafina

Serafina's blasphemous demand to have Rosario cremated shows her devotion and love. It demonstrates how far she will go to hold onto Rosario, even in death. Keeping him with her, inside her, beside her, all around her is the most important need of her life.

Serafina's speech is very sexual.

At night I sit here and I'm satisfied to remember . . . .

She doesn't say she is happy to remember but satisfied. Satisfaction is what the sexual experience is all about. Good sex is defined as satisfaction.

She continues with why she is satisfied.

Not the third best and not the second best, but the first best, the only best!

It is a good argument. Everything and everyone pales next to Rosario. Her belief is strong, almost ironclad. He was a loving man who fulfilled her in all areas of their relationship.

Serafina says she counts their nights, not counted, informing them she still counts, even now.

> *I count up the nights I held him all night in my arms, and I can tell you how many. Each night for twelve years. Four thousand—three hundred—and eighty.*

She knows the exact number of days. She will not let go.

> *And I would feel cheap and degraded and not fit to live with my daughter or under the roof with the urn of his blessed ashes, ...*

It is important she set a positive example for Rosa. She wants Rosa to respect and believe in true love.

Another reason for keeping the ashes on the mantle is to stay connected with Rosario. Two profoundly strong motivations to keep her rooted in the past.

Her humorous vision of the possibilities out there keeps her clutching to her love for Rosario.

> *... some other, some middle-aged man, not young, not full of young passion, but getting a pot belly on him and losing his hair and smelling of sweat and liquor ....*

Finally, Serafina, in defiance, sets up the love and belief that will have to be penetrated in order for her to move forward in her life.

> *I'm satisfied to remember the love of a man that was mine—only mine! Never touched by the hand of* nobody! Nobody *but* me!—*Just me! Never nobody but me!*

Serafina screams for someone to awaken her from the emotional paralysis she has locked herself in. It has become her own prison. Unbeknownst to her conscious mind, she wants out. This speech is a scream for help to be freed from her grip on the past. On the surface, Serafina seems content to remain in the past with Rosario. The truth is the opposite of what she is saying. A person who has experienced this intense passion wants it again.

Her monologue has passion, insight, love, humor, obsession, and conviction.

Beneatha

Beneatha begins by asking Asagai a simple question, repeating it, then turning it into a statement.

> *Me? ... Me? ... Me ....*

She concludes by discovering what she thinks of herself.

> *I'm nothing.*

Hearing her self-description causes her to take a breath and utter her next word.

> *Me.*

This simple, six-word opening informs us she has lost herself. Her dreams and beliefs no longer keep her together. These words are a cry for help. She needs Asagai to convince her that her ideals are right. She needs him to help her restore her faith in herself.

Beneatha recalls the moment her life took on a greater meaning. She recalls Rufus.

> *A kid named Rufus came down too fast ....*

She feels like Rufus now.

> *I remember standing there looking at his bloody open face thinking that was the end of Rufus.*

She sits there feeling she is at life's end. Raw and completely open to another human being, she is experiencing this vulnerability for the first time in her young adult life.

> *... and the next time I saw Rufus he just had a little line down the middle of his face ... I never got over that ... That that was what one person could do for another, fix him up—sew up the problem, make him all right again.*

Reliving this moment in her life Beneatha rekindles her feelings about the medical profession and the miracles she believed it could accomplish. This is what she wanted to be part of.

> *... it doesn't seem deep enough, close enough to what ails mankind! It was a child's way of seeing things—or an idealists's.*

Awakening to these feelings again brings back the pain caused by the loss of the money. She needs to defend herself against the pain and find a way to move on with her life.

Her monologue shows despair, numbness, fear, awakening, idealism, and cynicism.

Peter

Peter arrives furious, incensed, and unhappy with Heidi. She has no time for him. She informs him she is able to separate her feelings from her physical need for Scoop. Peter realizes Heidi invests herself in sex, art, and feminism but puts little importance on emotional relationships. Peter blurts out his discovery of Heidi.

> *What a perky Seventies kind of gal you are!*

He is angry that she still allows Scoop to use her for his own needs. She has lost herself to her beliefs and ideology.

> *... if you tell me you secrete endorphins when you run, ...*

In other words, he wonders if she has completely turned into Scoop.

Peter tells Heidi about his life. His homosexuality. His relationship with Stanley Zinc. His sharing of his life with another person. He wants her to understand its importance. Peter needs to awaken Heidi to the emotionally empty life she is headed for. He wants her to focus on the current path she is on. He cares for and loves her, and he wants a deeper emotional life for her.

Heidi's preoccupation keeps her separated from Peter until he is forced to reveal his most intimate truth three times. Finally, he asks her a question to make sure she gets it.

> *Heidi, I'm gay, okay?*

He uses humor, honesty, and patience, something he has very little of in this moment. She doesn't seem to get it. He keeps trying. He finally blurts out what he wants from her.

> *I am demanding your equal time and consideration.*

This word demanding, not asking, shows the escalation of his need. Heidi doesn't hear Peter, forcing him to press forward to get her to listen. The importance of his objective deepens.

Finally he says, "*I am demanding,*" not asking but demanding.

Every clue is information you uncover through plumbing the text. These clues help you specify each moment. This in-depth examination of your text brings out the detailed truth.

4

Using the Actor's Tools

Actors have tools for creating a character. These tools aid in forming the inner workings of the character. The tools are not in your character's consciousness. They are the brushes and oils of the painter. The notes and rests of the composer. The ideas and words of the writer. When you hear music, read a book, or look at a painting, you are not aware of how the piece was put together; you do not see the work. It appears seamless, just as your character must appear in front of her audience.

A character is created by layering. Layers of beliefs, ideas, and fears just as they exist within you. A psychiatrist works with a patient to remove layers of neurosis to get to his true self. Imagine an onion being peeled layer by layer until arriving at its very core. You, the actor, add each layer, starting with the true self, to create the intricacy of your character's psyche. It is the reverse of the analyst's process and ends with the complete person covered by a protective outer skin.

Using these actor's tools, each added to the previous one, creates layers of complex humanity. Each layer reveals something new about your character. Each tool, personally perceived, brings its own value to fulfilling your interpretation.

None of these tools are to be taken for granted. None should be overlooked. Each serves a definite and specific purpose in fully realizing your character. The actor's tools lead you to an organically spontaneous, three-dimensional human being living in the moment for the first time.

Involving Your Awareness

Awareness is the actor's greatest gift. Everything begins with your awareness acting in tandem with your instinct; it awakens you to personal and emotional effects created by people, places, and things. Your awareness connects you with these effects. It is sharpened through a process of self-exploration.

Tune into your awareness. Begin awakening to the effects you experience. The stronger effects permeate your consciousness. The subtler ones often occur without your registering them. Each person's awareness affects him or her differently. The greater the connection with your awareness, the more detailed and personal your character.

Awaken to your response. to pain or joy, receiving good or bad news. Interacting with people, places, and objects. Experience your feelings in different weather. Keep examining. Observe the subtle effects of different colors. Allow yourself to become aware of the effects of others' behavior, habits, idiosyncrasies, and their effects on you.

Become aware of everything affecting your life. Know how you feel about politics, religion, sex, or abortion. All things—as simple as color, as complicated as religion—add to the range of variety and specific choices in developing your character.

Your first cup of coffee in the morning arouses your senses. First comes your sense of smell. Then, you feel the warmth on your hands, face, and nose. Visually you respond to the color. Become aware of the effects on each of your senses, and you will understand the many moments of awakening before you taking your first sip.

Edmund

Edmund is outdoors talking to Nature who is all around him. While presenting his case, he becomes aware of changes in the air, the rustling of the leaves. All Nature's signs to him.

In his hand he holds the letter to his father. There are ever changing sensations in his hand as the letter passes from being a piece of parchment to the key to his future.

This awareness keeps Edmund involved and alive, connecting him with the immediate, moving him from one action to the next. His awareness of the letter is ever present.

Serafina

Serafina's home is sacred to her. Flora and Bessie's presence make her aware of the sanctity she feels there and of her need to protect both Our Lady and Rosario's ashes from their ribald chatter and actions. The women alert her to both the emptiness and respect she experiences. Their shallowness awakens an awareness of her own propriety, even in her underdressed and disheveled condition.

Flora's threat of exposure arouses Serafina's need for security, both for herself and for Rosa.

Beneatha

Beneatha's awareness of her vulnerability is heightened by the presence of Asagai. She chooses to allow herself to remain undefended to his scrutiny. Watching his every reaction to the details, she discovers the truth and the depth of her desire to become a doctor.

Beneatha's intense awareness of Asagai's support allows her to remain emotionally open in the moment.

Peter

Peter's awareness of the vast open space and the people around him causes him to focus intently on Heidi. Her inability to hear what he has to say raises his awareness of her preoccupation and her lack of interest in him and their friendship, driving him to demand her full attention. His awareness of these issues increases the importance of getting through to her. His awareness of her preoccupation and disinterest introduces him to new and disturbing facets of her personality.

Trusting Your Instinct

Your instinct is your divining rod to the truth. Trust in the power and direction offered by your instinct. It allows you to bring your personal truth to your character. Your instinct is your core, the very essence of what makes you unique and original.

Your instinct is a spark impelling you to respond and take action. It sets your work apart from others by creating honesty and originality. Artists use blues and reds, but how they instinctively use them creates their uniqueness. The same holds true for actors.

Your palette is a variety of instinctual emotional responses stemming from the effects of objects, places, and/or other people. The choice of actions you take to achieve your objective creates a variety of emotional colors. Your choices create a unique character no other actor can duplicate in exactly the same combination. Much like your fingerprint, it is yours specifically.

Instinctive reactions to a monologue or a moment should be paid attention to. Feel these sparks. Live with them. Experience them through your entire body. Try not to run them through your brain. Your brain dulls their effects, forcing you to question their validity.

Instinctive responses are visceral. The more viscerally you express your choices, the greater impact on your audience.

Keeping It Simple

Keeping it simple is just what the phrase implies. The more words used to explain simplicity, the more complicated it becomes. Being simple and instinctual in your choices and actions creates a clearly defined, multilayered character. Simplicity brings complexity, mystery, and surprise.

Simplicity creates clarity, which allows your audience to experience your character's actions, needs, and emotional journey. Clarity in creating steps toward your character's emotional journey communicates her need to achieve her objective.

Creating Complexity vs. Complication

Complication differs from complexity. Complications exist in your character's situation and circumstance. Complicating your character's needs muddies his inner life. It causes misinformation and creates a difficulty in your believing his truth.

Creating a multilayered, complex character action is achieved with the use of simple choices. Fulfilled actions simply taken

create detailed moments, allowing your audience to fully understand the truth and honesty of your character's needs. Complications create opaqueness that releases the audience from
feeling the depth of your character's needs. Simplicity brings a
translucency, involving the audience in your character's emotional journey. Layering each aspect of your character's needs,
actions, and motivations creates complexity.

The character's situation and circumstances created by the
author are, in most instances, complicated. Your character works
through these complications to get to her truth. Truth and honesty are achieved through simplicity. The more simply your character's truth and honesty are communicated to the audience the
greater the recognition.

Simplicity creates clear and insightful universal feelings.
Universality creates a personal union between your character and
the audience allowing it to experience its own feelings about the
events and issues in the moment.

Keeping your choices simple aids in trusting your instinct.
Accept your instinctive choices. Intellectualizing releases your
audience from your emotional grasp and allows it to think, not
feel, about your character. You want to keep your audience in the
moment, commingling their feelings with your character's. You
don't want to allow them to get into their heads and think their
emotions. You want to take them along with you and have them
experience their feelings in the moment.

Edmund

Edmund's world, situation, and circumstance are complicated. His
needs are complex. Trust the simple power of his needs to hold
the audience's interest. His need for acceptance is a universal
motivating force. Allowing the audience to comprehend his
needs carries it on his moment-by-moment emotional journey.

Edmund's illegitimacy makes him feel less than his brother
Edgar. His complexity comes from not understanding why he has
to suffer the pain of his father's actions. He believes this illegitimate union has created a stronger and more powerful person. He
knows he has done nothing to deserve this treatment, but he cannot help suffering from its effects.

Edmund gets down to basics in his talk with Nature, his goddess.

> *... For that I am some twelve or fourteen moonshines*
> *Lag of a brother? Why bastard? Wherefore base?*
> *When my dimensions are as well compact*
> *My mind as generous, and my shape as true,*
> *As honest madam's issue?*

I am as good as Edgar, he says. There is no reason for the treatment I receive from my father and society. He needs to stop his excruciating emotional pain. Putting his plan into action causes him greater turmoil. He will never be certain Nature has sided with him. Subconsciously, he is always unsure that he made the right choice, which deepens his complexity.

By consciously revealing his complex needs to Nature, he feels she understands his humanity and motivation. His actions complicate his already complicated situation.

Serafina

Serafina believes in the love she shared with Rosario. At the same time, she blocks out the truth of his philandering with Estelle Hohengarten. The depth of her need to believe and to cling to her past is her protective shell. She combats negative thoughts about what might have been. Clutching onto her beliefs while pushing away other truths brings complexity.

Serafina's complexity is revealed through her protestations of not wanting love to reenter her life while expressing her profound need for Rosario's love, which reveals her longing. The audience feels the depth of her need. Her desire to feel love in her life again is expressed subliminally. It enlightens her soul. She believes in love. The audience roots for her to awaken and experience that feeling once again.

As each trait and contradiction is layered onto Serafina, she becomes clearer and more complex. Mysterious but not indecipherable. Surprising and yet understandable.

Beneatha

Beneatha is a complex woman appearing to be simple and direct. She is ahead of her time—an awakening feminist African

American woman in the early 1950s studying medicine and blazing new trails. Luckily, she has the support of her mother. Her simple directness protects her from a world unable to understand her complexities.

Beneatha's complexity presents itself through her veneer of humor. The audience experiences her needs through the humor, which reveals her true desires and objectives.

Being devastated by Walter Lee's actions brings out her true warmth and vulnerability. Returning to the moment she made her life's decision reveals the profound and simple truth behind her complexities. Rufus's accident reawakens her primal need to care for and heal humanity. She cannot allow the newly complicated circumstances to shortchange her life.

In the opening moments of her speech to Asagai, she simply allows herself to experience her feelings of defeat. Action by action, moment by moment, she rebuilds herself into the woman with the dreams and ideals the audience has come to know. Simplicity allows it to clearly understand the complex woman underneath the clown she uses as a defense against the world's injustices. She gets the audience to care and to root for her to restore and fulfill her dreams.

Peter

Peter appears to be a secure and focused person living in a politically complicated time. The president of the United States is resigning, and women are fighting for equality. His need for Heidi to accept him reveals the complexity beneath his persona. He needs her to understand that their personal and platonic relationship is as important as her political and ideological beliefs.

Peter's sexual preference adds its own complexity. He is a man in conflict. He loves Heidi. He is gay. He wants Heidi's love and respect. He knows it is something he can have only platonically. He wishes things could be different. Heidi's involvement with Scoop adds another layer of complications.

These are the complexities in the four characters. Complexities create characters with multilayered personalities living in their specific styles. Simplicity reveals the depth of their truth, involving the audience in their personal inner conflicts. Simplicity adds surprises by uncovering your character's subconscious, layer by layer.

Deciding on an Objective

The objective is the actor's most important tool. It is the foundation of your work, the spine of your character. The character's need to reach his objective creates focus activating each moment. Exploring the material and understanding your character's behavior defines his emotional truth. This truth, both consciously and unconsciously, reveals insight into his specific needs. This detailed examination affirms the knowledge, instinctively perceived, leading to your choice of the correct life-and-death objective.

What your character needs from the other person is her objective. Know what your character wants the other person to do when she is finished speaking. Specifically how you want the other person to react creates focus. Do you want the other person to kiss you? Kick you? Walk out on you? Take you in their arms and console you? The specific answers to these questions are what your character doggedly pursues, forming her objective.

Like many people, characters often have no conscious idea of what they want. Through emotional denial, suppression, or repression, and often different combinations of all three, they are left in the dark as to their own emotional needs and truth. Exploration leads you to the dark recesses in your character's truth.

Characters' needs to fulfill their objective creates their emotional journey. Moving moment to moment, taking one action at a time moves your characters from one emotional place to another, creating both emotional movement and change.

Love, money, power, and sex are powerful motivators. Money, power, and sex become the covers hiding your character's need for love. Explore, and you will find money buys love. Power attracts people. Sex is seeking love from or power over another person. Understand your character's feelings and need for love. Its redemptive power. Its destructive power. Its fulfilling power. A choice to live without it is about love. Possibly the fear of love can cause hurt and pain from abandonment. Characters are motivated by love.

Examine your feelings about love. Sharing personal insights allows your audience to connect emotionally with its own intimate feelings. Your character's need to reach his objective emotionally connects with your audience.

The objective creates the motivation for your character's moment-to-moment actions. It creates the importance of the other person. The other person, the person your character is talking to, holds the key to fulfilling his objective. This importance arouses your character's awareness to the other person's reactions. Tracking him every moment, reading his every reaction to your character's words and actions makes your character alive in the moment.

The objective is like the trunk of a tree. Everything is attached to the trunk. Your chosen actions specify your character's need. The objective creates her behavior, motivations and driving force.

An objective of life and death importance creates immediacy and urgency that compels the audience's attention and involvement. The greater the importance and urgency, the wider your variety of choices. The objective needs to be felt and experienced throughout your character's being, inhabiting her body, soul, and mind. Feel and sense this importance. Don't intellectualize it. Don't think about it. It needs to be visceral, making your character tingle with life and expressing her emotional nakedness.

Throughout the monologue there are clues to your character's emotional state and needs. Examine them. Explore their meaning. Look for justification of these clues throughout the text. Rereading the text brings new and important aspects to your character's being.

Edmund

Reading and exploring *King Lear*, the importance of Edmund's need to be loved becomes evident. On the surface, his plan appears cold and greedy. Look further, and you discover a wounded and vulnerable soul desperately in need of love and justified in his actions.

Just before his death he says:

Yet Edmund was beloved.

This moment reveals the depth of his need, expressing the inner conflict that propelled his actions. His acceptance that Goneril poisoned her sister Regan for his love and then killed herself confirms this realization.

The objective, then, is to get Nature to give him a simple and direct signal to move forward with his plan to gain his father's love as well as his rightful title and estate.

Serafina

Serafina has convinced herself to remain in the past. Her grip on the past stops life's inevitable forward movement. She demonstrates the depth of her need by taking defiant actions. She believes Rosario's ashes will keep her love alive forever.

Her powerful protestations and belief in the truth and love she shared with Rosario offers a "Methinks the lady doth protest too much" feeling about her needs. Unconsciously, the opposite of her words seems to be the truth in the moment.

Her objective is to get Flora and Bessie to penetrate her protective shell and open her to life's infinite possibilities.

Beneatha

Beneatha's confidence has been shaken by Walter Lee's actions. For the first time, she is unsure of everything she believed. She is like a wounded deer confronted by bright lights.

Talking to Asagai, she exposes herself as she never would with her family. Asagai makes her feel safe. He believes in her dreams.

For the first time, Beneatha needs assurance to convince her that she is on the right path.

Her objective is to get Asagai to affirm and restore her faith in her dreams.

Peter

Heidi's impenetrable preoccupation with her feminist cause and self-protection fuels Peter's need to get through to her. His realization of Heidi's inability to hear him forces him to demand her attention. Peter is alarmed at Heidi's unwillingness to see her own lack of personal and emotional growth.

His objective is to get Heidi to acknowledge the importance of their relationship.

A life and death objective places your character in a vulnerable place forcing him to take emotional risks. This creates a tightrope for him to walk. You know the outcome, but your character, alive only in the moment, does not.

Never stop fighting to achieve your objective. The objective grows more important and deepens from action to action in each moment. Your character moves forward beat by beat, believing he will achieve his objective. He fights to the end.

Know specifically how your character wants the other person to respond. This knowledge focuses your actions toward reaching your objective.

5

Taking the Emotional Journey

The objective fueled by actions creates emotional movement. This movement is your character's emotional journey. Your character travels his or her emotional journey, beginning in one emotional place and arriving at another. The audience shares this journey by empathizing with and understanding your character's needs and beliefs. Communicating these needs and beliefs, simply and specifically, gets the audience to root for your character to reach his or her objective.

Edmund

Edmund begins in an angst-ridden, time-pressured, obsessive emotional state. He is desperate to feel good about himself. He calls on Nature and expresses his urgent need for help. He needs to be assured of his equality with his brother and his own worthiness to inherit his father's title and estate.

He begins his journey by expressing his commitment to Nature.

> *Thou, Nature, art my goddess; to thy law my services are bound.*

He lays out the factual truth. He believes that the strength and power of his conception make him deserving of his father's title and estate. He needs Nature's affirmation to move forward with his plan, carrying him to self respect.

> *Edmund the base shall top th' legitimate. I grow, I*
> *prosper.*

He travels from his weakened, needy emotional state to empowerment by taking his emotional journey.

Serafina

Serafina begins her emotional journey accepting the contentment her love for Rosario brings her.

> *My folks was peasants, contadini, but he—he come*
> *from* land-*owners!* Signorille, *my husband!*

She tells Flora and Bessie how embedded their lives were and how deeply Rosario impacted her life.

She reawakens her sexual desires and protestingly denies any other truth.

> *I'm satisfied to remember the love of a man that*
> *was mine—*only mine! *Never touched by the hand*
> *of* nobody! Nobody *but me!—Just* me! *Never*
> *nobody but me!*

She travels from a state of emotional satisfaction to discontentment shown through protestations reflecting her need to remain in denial.

Beneatha

Beneatha begins her monologue in a state of total uncertainty. Her first words reveal where she lives emotionally in the moment.

> *Me? ... Me? ... Me, I'm nothing ....*

This uncertainty is new to her. Her dreams have vanished, and she feels she is nothing without them.

Unknowingly, she shares the origins of her dreams, carrying her and Asagai on an unexpected emotional journey of self-realization.

Beneatha begins emotionally bereft. Traveling into her past brings her to an enlightened, new place.

> *It was a child's way of seeing things—or an*
> *idealist's. . . .*

As an adult, she realizes her childhood dreams are, indeed, her basic human truth.

Peter

Peter's emotional journey begins in outrage covered with humor at Heidi's callousness. His frustration turns into comic rage at her pronouncement of her ability to compartmentalize her self.

> *What a perky Seventies kind of gal you are! You can*
> *separate sexual needs from emotional dependencies.*

Peter begins his journey upset with Heidi because of the emotional distance she creates between them. Revealing intimate details of his life to Heidi, he becomes more desperate to reach her.

> *I am demanding your equal time and consideration.*

Peter begins with humor-tinged concern and arrives at an even more disturbed state, demanding Heidi's attention.

Deciding on an objective and taking action toward reaching it move your character from one emotional place to another. By expressing his needs, your character takes an emotional journey giving his monologue an arc to travel through.

The emotional journey has awareness and discoveries. Sharing with the other person brings new emotional understanding. It involves and carries the audience along this trajectory, rooting for your character to reach his objective.

6

Breaking Down Your Script

Parsing into Beats

You have chosen an objective and are ready to begin work on the monologue. Your objective focuses the speech. Your character reaches his objective by moment-to-moment movement. Parsing your monologue into beats creates these moments.

A beat is a moment, a complete thought. It may be one word or a whole sentence. It may even be a breath. Just as a rest in music needs to be taken, the same with fulfilling this breath. A beat ends when you move to another thought. The more beats you create, the more specific your character's journey. Fulfill each beat by taking the necessary time to complete the thought before moving on to the next.

Breaking down your monologue into beats is like scoring a piece of music. Each note is completed before the next note is begun. Fulfilling each beat forces you to take your time. Beats cannot be rushed. You can fulfill a beat quickly, but you cannot rush through them.

Each character has her own way of thinking and speaking. Some characters speak in one-word beats and others in complete sentences. Look to the character for her truth. The way she speaks, her syntax and natural character rhythm, helps define the beats. The insight you bring to her emotional truth guides you to your character's behavioral patterns, leading to the correct beats. Your instinct is an important element in this part of the process.

Edmund

Thou, / Nature, / art my goddess; / to thy law my services are bound. / Wherefore / should I stand / in the plague of custom, / and permit / The curiosity of nations / to deprive me, / For / that I am / some twelve / or fourteen moonshines / Lag of a brother? / Why bastard? / Wherefore base, / When my dimensions are as well compact, / My mind as generous, / and / my shape as true, / As honest madam's issue? / Why brand they us / With base? / with baseness? / bastardy? base, / base? / Who, / in the lusty stealth of nature, / take More composition / and fierce quality / Than doth, / within / a dull, / stale, / tired bed, / Go to th' creating / a whole tribe of fops / Got 'tween asleep and wake? / Well then, / Legitimate / Edgar, / I must have your land. / Our father's love / is to the bastard / Edmund / As to th' legitimate. / Fine word, / "legitimate." / Well, / my legitimate, / if this letter speed / And / my invention thrive, / Edmund the base / Shall top th' legitimate. / I grow, / I prosper. / Now, / gods, / stand up for bastards! /

Serafina delle Rose

My folks was peasants, / contadini, / but he / —he come from land-owners! / Signorille, / my husband! / —At night / I sit here / and I'm satisfied to remember, / because I had the best. / —Not the third best / and not the second best, / but the first best, / the only best! / —So now / I stay here / and am satisfied now / to remember, ... / I count up the nights / I held him / all night / in my arms, / and / I can tell you how many. / Each night / for twelve years. / Four thousand —three hundred—

and eighty. / The number of nights / I held him / all night / in my arms. / Sometimes / I didn't sleep, / just held him / all night / in my arms. / And / I am satisfied with it. / I grieve for him. / Yes, / my pillow / at night's / never dry / —but I'm satisfied to remember. / And I would feel / cheap / and degraded / and / not fit to live with my daughter / or / under the roof with the urn of his blessed ashes, / those— / ashes of a rose / —if after that memory, / after knowing that man, / I went to some other, / some middle-aged man, / not young, / not full of young passion, / but getting a pot belly on him / and / losing his hair / and / smelling of sweat / and liquor / —and / trying to fool myself / that that / was love-making! / I know / what love-mak-ing was. / And I'm satisfied / just to remember / ... / Go on, / you do it, / you go on the streets / and let them drop their sacks of dirty water on you! / — I'm satisfied to remember / the love of a man / that was mine / —only mine! / Never touched / by the hand of nobody! / Nobody / but me! / — / Just me! / Never / nobody but me! /*

Beneatha

Me?... / Me?... / Me, / I'm nothing... / Me. / When I was very small / ... we used to take our sleds out / in the wintertime / and / the only hills we had / were the ice-covered stone steps / of some houses / down the street. / And we used to fill them in with snow / and make them smooth / and slide down them / all day / ... and it was very dangerous, / you know... / far too steep... / and sure enough / one day / a kid named Rufus / came down too fast / and hit the sidewalk / and we saw his face / just split open / right there in front of us / ...And I remember / standing there / looking at his bloody open face / thinking / that was the end of Rufus. /

*But / the ambulance came / and they took him to
the hospital / and they fixed the broken bones /
and they sewed it all up / . . . and the next time I
saw Rufus / he just had a little line down the middle of his face. . . / I never got over that / . . .That
that / was what one person could do for another, /
fix him up / —sew up the problem, / make him
all right again. / That was the most marvelous
thing in the world. . . / I wanted to do that. / I
always thought / it was the one concrete thing in
the world / that a human being could do. / Fix up
the sick, / you know / —and make them whole
again. / This was truly being God / . . .I wanted to
cure. / It used to be so important to me. / I wanted
to cure. / It used to matter / I used to care. / I mean
/ about people / and how their bodies hurt. . . / —
it doesn't seem deep enough, / close enough / to
what ails mankind! / It was a child's way / of seeing things / —or / an idealist's.*

Peter Patrone

*What a perky Seventies kind of gal you are! / You
can separate sexual needs / from emotional
dependencies. / Heidi, / if you tell me you secrete
endorphins when you run, / I'm going straight
into the curator's office / and demand an all
armor retrospective. / Actually, / I'm afraid I'm
feeling sort of distant from you. / I'm not criticizing you. / It's just how I'm feeling. / I haven't seen
you in eight months. / Heidi, / I don't play on your
team. / I've become a liberal homosexual pediatrician. / And I prefer Stanley. / My friend's name is
Stanley Zinc. / He's a child psychiatrist from Johns
Hopkins. / But / he's thinking of quitting / in
order to study with Merce Cunningham. / The sad
thing is / that Stanley is too old / to join the company / and / Miss Merce isn't getting any younger,*

either. / Anyway, / I'm thinking of replacing him / with a waiter I met last week, / we share a mutual distrust of Laura Nyro. / I would have told you all this earlier / but / I thought we deserved something more intimate / than a phone call. / So / I chose the Chicago Art Institute. / Heidi, / I'm gay, / okay? / I sleep with Stanley Zinc, M.D. / And my liberation, / my pursuit of happiness, / and / the pursuit of happiness of other men like me / is just as politically / and socially / valid / as hanging a couple of Goddamned paintings / because they were signed by someone named Nancy, / Gladys, / or Gilda. / And / that is why I came to see you today. / I am demanding your equal time / and consideration.

Applying Specifics

You have chosen your monologue. Decided on a life-and-death objective. Charted your character's emotional journey by parsing her monologue into beats. Before you go any further, it is important to understand the need for applying specifics. Specificity brings clarity in communicating with the other person, making it simpler to understand and relate to your character's behavior.

Specificity brings focus and universality to your work. Specifics create a more detailed character. As Anton Chekhov said, "The truth is in the details." Being specific adds complexity and clearly communicated insights to your character. The more specifically detailed your work, the greater the meaning communicated to your audience.

Specifics bring universal truth and honesty to your character. Generalities create maybes. Specifics create definitive moments. They focus on what your character is doing at each given moment. Generalities limit your range of choices and offer less defined characters.

"My character is about twenty-six" is general. You know exactly how old you are. Know this fact about your character. This will help you believe in your character. Being specific in all your choices compels your audience to be with you every moment of the emotional journey. Specifics offer you a wider range of choices. Variety creates a multilayered character.

Edmund

Thou, Nature, art my Goddess. . . .

Edmund calls on his specific and universal higher being or power.

. . .To thy law my services are bound.

This informs of his total commitment to her.

For that I am some twelve or fourteen moonshines
lag of a brother?

It is a specific reference to the difference in their ages: in such a short time, how could this chasm have been created between us for our father's love?

. . .My dimensions are as well compact, my mind
as generous and my shape as true as honest
madam's issue

Expressing his belief in their physical and mental equality, Edmund uses specifics to put these aspects into a proper, precise perspective.

Who, in the lusty stealth of nature, take
more composition and fierce quality
Than doth, within a dull, stale, tired bed,
Go to th' creating a whole tribe of fops
Got 'tween asleep and wake?

Edmund makes it specifically clear that he feels his father's illicit union created a man of fierce quality, laying out his stronger qualifications for inheriting Gloucester's title and estate.

The specifics communicate his reasons for believing he deserves to be loved, accepted, and the rightful heir apparent. These specifics make it clear he has thought long and hard about the issues before coming to beseech Nature for her help.

These specifics show Edmund's justification for deciding to give the letter to his father.

Serafina

> *My folks was peasants, contadini, but he—come from* land-*owners!*

This informs of the specific class difference between Serafina and Rosario. Specifying her respect for Rosario, she refuses to believe he lied about Estelle Hohengarten.

> *Not the third best and not the second best, but the* first *best, the* only *best!*

Serafina is very specific about the quality of their love and lovemaking.

> *Each night for twelve years. Four thousand—three hundred—and eighty. The number of nights I held him all night in my arms.*

She knows the number of years and the exact number of nights she held him in her arms.

> *And I would feel cheap and degraded and not fit to live with my daughter....*

Serafina is specific about the feelings she would experience if she had another man, informing the women she has thought about it and made a decision.

> ...*Some middle-aged man, not young, not full of young passion, but getting a pot belly on him and losing his hair and smelling of sweat and liquor....*

She has a very definite picture of the man awaiting her.

The specifics cited by Serafina justify her decision to remain in the past.

Beneatha

> *Me?... Me?... Me, I'm nothing ... Me.*

The specific need for the repetition of "Me" introduces us to Beneatha's numb emotional state. She doesn't move on. She chooses to remain and look for answers.

> ...*The only hills we had were the ice-covered stone steps of some houses down the street.*

This description paints a specific picture of where she played as a young girl. It also depicts the neighborhood and the economic background in just a few words.

> ...*and we saw his face just split open right there in front of us ... And I remember standing there looking at his bloody open face....*

The accident and the specific visual of Rufus have left an indelible impression on her. She can still see the split in his face and the exact color of the blood all over his face.

> ...*and the next time I saw Rufus he just had a little line down the middle of his face....*

She sees both the before and after images as vividly as if they were happening in the moment. The specifics of these images bring Asagai and the audience into the experience with her.

> *I always thought it was the one concrete thing in the world that a human being could do.*

The specific use of "concrete" shows the strength of her belief in the medical profession.

Peter

> *You can separate sexual needs from emotional dependencies.*

Peter recoils at the depth of Heidi's emotional compartmentalization.

> *I haven't seen you in eight months.*

He cites a specific length of time, a long time not to see an important friend.

> *I've become a liberal homosexual pediatrician.*

Peter uses three specific words to describe himself and so informs Heidi of his politics, sexuality, and profession, leaving nothing to conjecture.

> *My friend's name is Stanley Zinc. He's a child psychiatrist from Johns Hopkins.*

He tells Heidi about his boyfriend. He not only adds his profession but also the prestigious hospital where he works. These specifics reveal Peter's feelings of insecurity. Being involved with an important man will not only sell Heidi on Stanley but also allow her to accept his homosexuality.

> *And* my *liberation,* my *pursuit of happiness,* and
> *the pursuit of happiness of other men like me is*
> *just as politically and socially valid....*

Peter specifically informs Heidi where he stands morally, politically, and socially.

Specifics clarify each character's life, clearly defining what is important to each of them. They communicate to the other person and the audience the universal connection with all humanity. Specifics lift the character out of his limited environment, placing him on a larger universal playing field.

Igniting Impulses Through Actions

Acting teachers, coaches, and directors say, "acting is doing." Actions are the doing. This "doing" is an inner action creating the impetus for the resulting words your character uses to communicate with the other person. Actions ignite the impulse needed to move toward your objective.

Your character has an objective. Her monologue is parsed into beats. Reaching your character's objective needs actions for each beat. These actions activate your character in each moment. The actions create the movement your character takes on her emotional journey.

What is an *action*? There is confusion due to the many uses of the word. Actions are active verbs, i.e., to explain, to tell, to answer. Active verbs are used to create your character's inner life. They give your character an action to execute on each beat.

Actions are not to be confused with physical activities, often called physical actions or activities. Setting the table or baiting a fish hook are physical actions.

Think of a string of pearls, each separate but all connected. Like the pearls, each action needs to be separate and complete before moving to the next. Fulfilling each action creates clarity. Actions explain why your character chooses the specific words she does.

The actions are the how-to, how to achieve your objective. They are the actor's tools and not in the character's consciousness. Learn the actions, and the words will come. Once you learn your actions, forget them. Knowing what your character is doing at every moment brings forth the dialogue. The words are the result of the impulse ignited by the action.

Actions eliminate self-consciousness. Committing yourself to fulfilling your actions prevents you from doing anything else. Test this. Recall your first telephone number. As you concentrate on remembering, every other thought disappears.

Actions aid in keeping your character in the moment, establishing his subtext or inner dialogue, establishing his moment-to-moment reality, and keeping him moving along his emotional journey toward his objective.

The actions act as mini-objectives. Each action elicits a response from the other character. Specific knowledge of how you want the other character to react directs you in choosing the correct action. Remember, knowing specifically how you want the other person to react does not guarantee she will. That should not stop you from choosing this action. In the moment, your character does not know the other person's reaction until after she has taken the action.

Choose actions that focus on your objective. The actions may work together in a chosen sequence. For instance, choosing to make the other person laugh opens him to your next action, allowing him to hear what you need from him. The first action gets him to the more difficult moment when he hears what you need from him. Actions fulfill your character's needs and answer the question, "Why am I saying these words?"

Action speaks louder than words. This oft-repeated phrase will become clear when you begin examining other people's actions and observing that what they say is often different from what they do. Or vice versa. The actions express the truth. Words can be deceptive because the characters could be saying one thing while meaning another. Observe their actions. The words are the result of the ignited internal impulse. Think how you use words to camouflage truths. People can speak without revealing anything. The actions are the truth.

The well-known Shakespearean expression "Methinks the lady doth protest too much" definitively expresses this truth. Her actions are speaking louder than her words. She may be saying "no, no, no," but her actions are saying "yes, yes, yes." Look carefully, and discover how often the action is the true meaning.

Allow your instinct to guide you to the immediate and visceral action. Choose active verbs that strike a nerve and ignite a sensation internally.

These actions are an important step in your road map to creating a compelling performance.

Each chosen active verb should be simple. Simple actions combined, one following another, create a layered and complex person moving along the road toward her objective. Simple actions create clarity for the other characters and the audience to understand. Don't intellectualize the actions. Don't choose more complicated actions thinking they will make a more intelligent interpretation. Complicated actions cause lack of clarity, an opaqueness that cannot be followed. You will lose both the other character and the audience to their intellects. They will spend time trying to figure out what your character is doing. You want them to stay with you, feeling and experiencing fully every beat and moment you are creating.

Below is a list of sample active verbs:

To acknowledge	To greet
To agree	To guide
To ask	To inspire
To brag	To interrogate
To compliment	To mimic
To contradict	To seduce
To convince	To shame
To demonstrate	To strategize
To diffuse	To teach
To emphasize	To titillate
To explain	To trap

Here are the four monologues with actions, some from the list above, chosen specifically for the needs of each character's beats, objective, and clarity.

Edmund

> *Thou,*
>> To awaken
>
> *Nature,*
>> To name
>
> *art my goddess;*
>> To revere
>
> *to thy law*
>> To inform
>
> *My services are bound.*
>> To commit
>
> *Wherefore*
>> To begin
>
> *should I stand*
>> To ask
>
> *in the plague of custom,*
>> To define
>
> *and permit*
>> To state
>
> *The curiosity of nations*
>> To include
>
> *to deprive me,*
>> To explain
>
> *For*
>> To emphasize
>
> *that I am*
>> To pinpoint

some twelve
> To explain

or fourteen moonshines
> To correct

Lag of a brother?
> To define

Why bastard?
> To ask

Wherefore base,
> To demand

When my dimensions are as well compact,
> To explain

My mind as generous,
> To compliment

and
> To add

my shape as true,
> To compare

As honest madam's issue?
> To explain

Why brand they us with base?
> To question

with baseness?
> To search

bastardy?
> To declaim

base,
> To state

base?
> To question

Who,

        To seek

in the lusty stealth of nature,

        To specify

take more composition

        To add

and fierce quality

        To emphasize

Than doth,

        To confirm

within

        To define

a dull,

        To describe

stale,

        To color

tired bed,

        To malign

Go to th' creating

        To inform

a whole tribe of fops

        To define

Got 'tween asleep and wake?

        To specify

Well then,

        To warn

Legitimate

        To condemn

Edgar,

        To name

I must have your land.

To alert

Our father's love

To specify

is to the bastard

To inform

Edmund

To specify

As to th' legitimate.

To declare

Fine word,

To compliment

"legitimate."

To revel in

Well,

To enjoy

my legitimate,

To insult

if this letter speed

To explain

And

To discover

my invention thrive,

To relish

Edmund the base

To declare

Shall top th' legitimate.

To avenge

I grow,

To announce

I prosper.
>> To enjoy

Now,
>> To specify

gods,
>> To declare

stand up for bastards!
>> To demand

Serafina

My folks was peasants,
>> To share

contadini,
>> To define

but he—
>> To set apart

he come from land-*owners!*
>> To inform

Signorille,
>> To familiarize

my husband!
>> To extrapolate

—At night
>> To specify

I sit here
>> To describe

and I'm satisfied to remember,
>> To declare

because I had the best.—
>> To inform

—Not the third best
> To clarify

and not the second best,
> To emphasize

but the first *best,*
> To declare

the only best!
> To proclaim

—So now
> To continue

I stay here
> To inform

and am satisfied now
> To share

to remember, ...
> To conclude

I count up the nights
> To share

I held him
> To describe

all night
> To specify

in my arms,
> To explain

and
> To add

I can tell you how many.
> To inform

Each night
> To specify

for twelve years.

    To inform

Four thousand—three hundred—and eighty.

    To elaborate

The number of nights

    To explain

I held him

    To declare

all night

    To specify

in my arms.

    To describe

Sometimes

    To continue

I didn't sleep,

    To explain

just held him

    To emphasize

all night

    To define

in my arms.

    To inform

And

    To add

I am satisfied with it.

    To affirm

I grieve for him.

    To express

Yes,

    To acknowledge

my pillow

       To specify

at night's

       To define

never dry—

       To describe

but I'm satisfied to remember.

       To assure

And I would feel

       To share

cheap

       To explain

and degraded

       To disgust

and

       To emphasize

not fit to live with my daughter

       To confess

or

       To offer

under the roof with the urn of his blessed ashes,

       To define

Those—

       To specify

ashes of a rose—

       To revere

if after that memory,

       To clarify

after knowing that man,

       To pinpoint

I went to some other,

    To specify

some middle-aged man,

    To describe

not young,

    To define

not full of young passion,

    To inform

but getting a pot belly on him

    To paint

and

    To add

losing his hair

    To specify

and

    To continue

smelling of sweat

    To disgust

and liquor

    To exaggerate

—and

    To stress

trying to fool myself

    To inform

that that

    To focus

was love-making!

    To define

I know

    To inform

what love-making was.

To explain

And I'm satisfied

To share

just to remember

To explain

. . .

To pause

Go on,

To dismiss

you do it,

To prod

you go on the streets

To direct

and let them drop their sacks of dirty water on you!—

To encourage

I'm satisfied to remember

To inform

the love of a man

To share

that was mine—

To declare

only mine!

To stress

Never touched

To clarify

by the hand of nobody!

To define

Nobody

> To emphasize

but me!—

> To declare

Just me!

> To state

Never

> To reiterate

nobody but me!

> To proclaim

Beneatha

Me? . . .

> To ask

Me? . . .

> To ask

Me,

> To share

I'm nothing . . .

> To inform

Me.

> To acknowledge

When I was very small . . .

> To share

we used to take our sleds out

> To explain

in the wintertime

> To inform

and the only hills we had

> To define

were the ice-covered stone steps of some houses

To detail

down the street.

To specify

And we used to fill them in with snow

To explain

and make them smooth

To describe

and slide down them

To inform

all day . . .

To specify

and it was very dangerous,

To inform

you know . . .

To involve

far too steep . . .

To explain

and sure enough

To assure

one day

To recall

a kid named Rufus

To inform

came down too fast

To share

and hit the sidewalk

To inform

and we saw his face

To focus

just split open

　　　To describe

right there in front of us . . .

　　　To alarm

And I remember

　　　To recall

standing there

　　　To explain

looking at his bloody open face

　　　To share

thinking

　　　To seduce

that was the end of Rufus.

　　　To share

But

　　　To alert

the ambulance came

　　　To inform

and they took him to the hospital

　　　To share

and they fixed the broken bones

　　　To continue

and they sewed it all up . . .

　　　To explain

and the next time I saw Rufus

　　　To continue

he just had a little line down the middle of

his face . . .

  To describe

I never got over that . . .

  To share

That that

  To clarify

was what one person could do for another,

  To realize

fix him up—

  To explain

sew up the problem,

  To inform

make him all right again.

  To specify

That was the most marvelous thing in the world . . .

  To revel

I wanted to do that.

  To discover

I always thought

  To begin

it was the one concrete thing in the world

  To emphasize

that a human being could do.

  To explain

Fix up the sick,

  To clarify

you know—

  To penetrate

and make them whole again.

  To realize

This was truly being God . . .

>To state

I wanted to cure.

>To share

It used to be so important to me.

>To explain

I wanted to cure.

>To state

It used to matter.

>To inform

I used to care.

>To share

I mean

>To grab him

about people

>To explain

and how their bodies hurt

>To explain

. . .

>To ponder

it doesn't seem deep enough,

>To share

close enough

>To explain

to what ails mankind!

>To state

It was a child's way of seeing things—

>To dismiss

or

>To dramatize

an idealist's.

> To wrap up

Peter

What a perky Seventies kind of gal you are!

> To define

You can separate sexual needs

> To inform

from emotional dependencies.

> To declare

Heidi,

> To get her attention

if you tell me you secrete endorphins when you run,

> To confront

I'm going straight into the curator's office

> To inform

and demand an all armor retrospective.

> To define

Actually,

> To level

I'm afraid I'm feeling sort of distant from you.

> To inform

I'm not criticizing you.

> To clarify

It's just how I'm feeling.

> To explain

I haven't seen you in eight months.

> To inform

Heidi,

> To waken

I don't play on your team.

    To inform

I've become a liberal homosexual pediatrician.

    To declare

And

    To add

I prefer Stanley.

    To inform

My friend's name is Stanley Zinc.

    To include

He's a child psychiatrist from Johns Hopkins.

    To impress

But

    To grab her interest

he's thinking of quitting

    To share

in order to study with Merce Cunningham.

    To divert

The sad thing is

    To inform

that Stanley is too old

    To state

to join the company

    To inform

and

    To further

Miss Merce isn't getting any younger, either.

    To amuse

Anyway,

    To change the subject

I'm thinking of replacing him

> To pique her interest

with a waiter I met last week,

> To inform

we share a mutual distrust of Laura Nyro.

> To inform

I would have told you all this earlier

> To inform

but

> To control

I thought we deserved something more intimate

> To explain

than a phone call.

> To share

So

> To inform

I chose the Chicago Art Institute.

> To amuse

Heidi,

> To get her attention

I'm gay,

> To reveal

okay?

> To ask

I sleep with Stanley Zinc, M.D.

> To inform

And my *liberation,*

> To define

my *pursuit of happiness,*

> To specify

and *the pursuit of happiness of other men like me*

>To inform

is just as politically

>to explain

and socially

>To add

valid

>to declare

as hanging a couple of Goddamned paintings

>To compare

because they were signed by someone named Nancy,

>To specify

Gladys,

>To add

or Gilda.

>To press the point

And

>To hold her attention

that is why I came to see you today.

>To inform

I am demanding your equal time

>To express

and consideration.

>To close

Coloring with Adjustments

You ask a question and get no answer. You ask again, speaking louder. Same result. You take a deep breath and enunciate more clearly. Still nothing. Frustrated, you ask with impatience in your voice. Finally. An answer.

Each time you asked the question, you made an adjustment. First, you asked the question in a straightforward, direct manner. Assuming she did not hear you, you ask louder. Thinking you may have mumbled, you enunciate with more precision. Finally, your frustration and annoyance colors the question with impatience. This time you get your answer. You asked the same question four times, coloring with adjustments to make each different. Adjustments modify the actions, giving your actions specificity.

You choose an action. By itself, it is general, ripe for interpretation, asking for direction to its execution. You modify the action by adding an adjustment directing you toward a specific interpretation. Adjustments are specifically chosen to guide your character toward getting what he wants. They are subtle but important to your work. They modify beats, words, and moments and affect your emotional state. They express your character's feeling in every moment. Adjustments color your actions.

Explore moments in your life to understand and feel the subtle difference in adjustments. The moment you heard you got the part or got an A on a paper. These are moments that made you feel good about yourself. Now choose a moment where you failed, and felt bad. Examine these contrasting moments. Experience the emotional difference: the exhilaration of joy and the angst and sadness of defeat. Adjustments are never arbitrary.

Subtlety and nuance occur when you fulfill your adjusted actions. Each adjustment adds a new dimension that reveals your character's true feelings. Coloring with adjustments varies your monologue.

Adjustments may change your character's rhythm. An exciting event quickens her internal movement. Sad or depressing moments bring on lethargy, slowing her down. Again, these are subtle differences, but they add an element of change and variety.

Often you will find yourself choosing the same action consecutively on a series of beats. Adjustments subtly color each action making them different. There is a subtle difference between mauve and lilac. They are similar yet different; each is a specific shade of purple. This is the specificity and variety adjustments bring to your work.

Edmund

Edmund's actions are adjusted by his feelings toward Edgar. They bring colors of jealousy, resentment, or anger depending on your specific choice. The choice is specific to Edmund in the moment and needs to be explored through your personal perspective.

Explore your complex feelings toward your own siblings. You love them, and yet there are moments filled with hate. The hate does not preclude the love. It often enhances the love. You only hate those you love. If you like, you create dislike. The person you like does not involve you enough to hate.

Thou,

> To awaken (*immediately*)

Nature,

> To name (*specifically*)

art my goddess;

> To revere (*openly*)

to thy law

> To inform (*definitively*)

My services are bound.

> To commit (*completely*)

Wherefore

> To begin (*openly*)

should I stand

> To ask (*directly*)

in the plague of custom,

> To define (*specifically*)

and permit

> To state (*openly*)

The curiosity of nations

> To include (*definitively*)

to deprive me,

> To explain (*personally*)

For

      To emphasize (*dramatically*)

that I am

      To pinpoint (*specifically*)

some twelve

      To explain (*warmly*)

or fourteen moonshines

      To correct (*specifically*)

Lag of a brother?

      To define (*questioningly*)

Why bastard?

      To ask (*truthfully*)

Wherefore base,

      To demand (*questioningly*)

When my dimensions are as well compact,

      To explain (*flatteringly*)

My mind as generous,

      To compliment (*superiorly*)

and

      To add (*pointedly*)

my shape as true,

      To compare (*honestly*)

As honest madam's issue?

      To explain (*snidely*)

Why brand they us with base?

      To question (*humorously*)

with baseness?

      To search (*angrily*)

bastardy?

      To declaim (*angrily*)

base,

> To state (*quizzically*)

base?

> To question (*ironically*)

Who,

> To seek (*imploringly*)

in the lusty stealth of nature,

> To specify (*directly*)

take more composition

> To specify (*pointedly*)

and fierce quality

> To emphasize (*personally*)

Than doth,

> To confirm (*proudly*)

within

> To define (*specifically*)

a dull,

> To describe (*happily*)

stale,

> To color (*nastily*)

tired bed,

> To malign (*humourously*)

Go to th' creating

> To inform (*joyfully*)

a whole tribe of fops

> To define (*outrageously*)

Got 'tween asleep and wake?

> To specify (*factually*)

Well then,

> To warn (*carefully*)

Legitimate

      To condemn (*disgustedly*)

Edgar,

      To name (*specifically*)

I must have your land.

      To alert (*warningly*)

Our father's love

      To specify (*inclusively*)

is to the bastard

      To inform (*harshly*)

Edmund

      To specify (*definitively*)

As to th' legitimate.

      To declare (*strongly*)

Fine word,

      To compliment (*appreciatively*)

"legitimate."

      To revel in (*horrifyingly*)

Well,

      To enjoy (*openly*)

my legitimate,

      To insult (*snidely*)

if this letter speed

      To explain (*definitely*)

And

      To discover (*gleefully*)

my invention thrive,

      To relish (*savoringly*)

Edmund the base

      To declare (*proudly*)

Shall top th' legitimate.
> To avenge (*happily*)

I grow,
> To announce (*loudly*)

I prosper.
> To enjoy (*joyfully*)

Now,
> To specify (*immediately*)

gods,
> To declare (*inclusively*)

stand up for bastards!
> To demand (*willfully*)

Serafina

Serafina's speech is filled with profound love and extreme sexual satisfaction. Explore your own emotions in both areas. Allow yourself to make personal and specific choices in choosing her adjustments.

My folks was peasants
> To share (*informatively*)

contadini,
> To define (*specifically*)

But he—
> To set apart (*specially*)

he come from land-*owners!*
> To inform (*impressively*)

Signorille,
> To familiarize (*reverentially*)

my husband!
> To translate (*intelligently*)

—At night
> To specify (*romantically*)

I sit here

      To describe (*specifically*)

and I'm satisfied to remember,

      To declare (*openly*)

because I had the best.—

      To inform (*lovingly*)

Not the third best

      To clarify (*pointedly*)

and not the second best,

      To emphasize (*specifically*)

but the first *best,*

      To declare (*definitively*)

the only *best!*

      To proclaim (*proudly*)

—So now

      To continue (*freshly*)

I stay here

      To inform (*clearly*)

and am satisfied now

      To share (*contentedly*)

to remember, ...

      To conclude (*lovingly*)

I count up the nights

      To share (*happily*)

I held him

      To describe (*tenderly*)

all night

      To specify (*lovingly*)

in my arms,

      To explain (*intimately*)

and

> To add (*joyfully*)

I can tell you how many.

> To inform (*proudly*)

Each night

> To specify (*clearly*)

for twelve years.

> To inform (*definitively*)

Four thousand—three hundred—and eighty.

> To elaborate (*joyfully*)

The number of nights

> To explain (*factually*)

I held him

> To declare (*factually*)

all night

> To specify (*lovingly*)

in my arms.

> To describe (*warmly*)

Sometimes

> To continue (*informingly*)

I didn't sleep,

> To explain (*enjoyably*)

just held him

> To emphasize (*specifically*)

all night

> To define (*simply*)

in my arms.

> To inform (*sensually*)

And

> To add (*gloatingly*)

I am satisfied with it.

    To affirm (*acceptingly*)

I grieve for him.

    To express (*sharingly*)

Yes,

    To acknowledge (*sadly*)

my pillow

    To specify (*rememberingly*)

at night's

    To define (*factually*)

never dry—

    To describe (*proudly*)

but I'm satisfied to remember.

    To assure (*definitely*)

And I would feel

    To share (*openly*)

cheap

    To explain (*pointedly*)

and degraded

    To disgust (*informingly*)

and

    To emphasize (*importantly*)

not fit to live with my daughter

    To confess (*revealingly*)

or

    To offer (*discouragingly*)

under the roof with the urn of his blessed ashes,

    To define (*piously*),

those

    To specify (*assuredly*)

—ashes of a rose—

      To revere (*lovingly*)

if after that memory,

      To clarify (*markedly*)

after knowing that man,

      To pinpoint (*definitively*)

I went to some other,

      To specify (*astonishedly*)

some middle-aged man,

      To describe (*factually*)

not young,

      To define (*clearly*)

not full of young passion,

      To inform (*disparagingly*)

but getting a pot belly on him

      To paint (*exaggeratedly*)

and

      To add (*joyfully*)

losing his hair

      To specify (*humorously*)

and

      To continue (*knowingly*)

smelling of sweat

      To disgust (*overtly*)

and liquor

      To exaggerate (*disgustedly*)

—and

      To stress (*emphatically*)

trying to fool myself

      To inform (*truthfully*)

that that

       To focus (*directly*)

was love-making!

       To define (*ridiculously*)

I know

       To inform (*definitively*)

what love-making was.

       To explain (*informingly*)

And I'm satisfied

       To share (*happily*)

just to remember

       To explain (*lovingly*)

. . .

       To pause (*deliberately*)

Go on,

       To dismiss (*directly*)

you do it,

       To prod (*defyingly*)

you go on the streets

       To direct (*descriptively*)

and let them drop their sacks of dirty water on you!—

       To encourage (*ironically*)

I'm satisfied to remember

       To inform (*proudly*)

the love of a man

       To share (*joyfully*)

that was mine—

       To declare (*triumphantly*)

only mine!

> To stress (*pointedly*)

Never touched

> To clarify (*warningly*)

by the hand of nobody!

> To define (*definitively*)

Nobody

> To emphasize (*emphatically*)

but me!—

> To declare (*purely*)

Just me!

> To state (*simply*)

Never

> To reiterate (*pointedly*)

nobody but me!

> To proclaim (*defiantly*)

Beneatha

Beneatha's speech begins in a vulnerably open and emotional-ly bereft space moving to a protective cynicism. During her emotional journey, she is awestruck, awakened, horrified, humor-ous, bitter, angry, proud, and accepting. Find within you the moment of your lowest emotional point. Live in this vulnerable truth as you choose your adjustments.

Me? . . .

> To ask (*blankly*)

Me? . . .

> To ask (*questioningly*)

Me,

> To share (*factually*)

I'm nothing ...

> To inform (*triumphantly*)

Me.

> To acknowledge (*ironically*)

When I was very small ...

> To share (*informatively*)

we used to take our sleds out

> To explain (*descriptively*)

in the wintertime

> To inform (*specifically*)

and the only hills we had

> To define (*informatively*)

were the ice-covered stone steps of some houses

> To detail (*descriptively*)

down the street.

> To specify (*informatively*)

And we used to fill them in with snow

> To explain (*actively*)

and make them smooth

> To describe (*comfortingly*)

and slide down them

> To inform (*entertainingly*)

all day ...

> To specify (*rememberingly*)

and it was very dangerous,

> To inform (*factually*)

you know ...

> To involve (*understandingly*)

far too steep ...

> To explain (*dangerously*)

and sure enough
> To assure (*affirmingly*)

one day
> To recall (*specifically*)

a kid named Rufus
> To inform (*introductorily*)

came down too fast
> To share (*frighteningly*)

and hit the sidewalk
> To inform (*pointedly*)

and we saw his face just split open
> To focus (*shockingly*)

right there in front of us . . .
> To alarm (*horrifically*)

And I remember
> To recall (*thoughtfully*)

standing there
> To explain (*numbingly*)

looking at his bloody open face
> To share (*amazingly*)

thinking
> To seduce (*mysteriously*)

that was the end of Rufus.
> To share (*realizingly*)

But
> To alert (*sharingly*)

the ambulance came
> To inform (*carefully*)

and they took him to the hospital
> To share (*awkwardly*)

and they fixed the broken bones

>To continue (*amazingly*)

and they sewed it all up ...

>To explain (*unbelievingly*)

and the next time I saw Rufus

>To continue (*informingly*)

he just had a little line down the middle of his face ...

>To describe (*surprisedly*)

I never got over that ...

>To share (*effectively*)

That that

>To clarify (*awkwardly*)

was what one person could do for another,

>To realize (*discoveringly*)

fix him up—

>To explain (*amazingly*)

sew up the problem,

>To inform (*definitively*)

make him all right again.

>To specify (*clearly*)

That was the most marvelous thing in the world ...

>To revel (*discoveringly*)

I wanted to do that.

>To discover (*awakeningly*)

I always thought

>To begin (*realizingly*)

it was the one concrete thing in the world

>To emphasize (*definitively*)

that a human being could do.

       To explain (*profoundly*)

Fix up the sick,

       To clarify (*explicitly*)

you know—

       To penetrate (*attentively*)

and make them whole again.

       To realize (*deeply*)

This was truly being God . . .

       To state (*factually*)

I wanted to cure.

       To share (*fantasizingly*)

It used to be so important to me.

       To explain (*clearly*)

I wanted to cure.

       To state (*truthfully*)

It used to matter.

       To inform (*honestly*)

I used to care.

       To share (*importantly*)

I mean

       To grab him (*attentively*)

about people

       To explain (*specifically*)

and how their bodies hurt

       To explain (*painfully*)

. . .

       To ponder (*decidedly*)

it doesn't seem deep enough,

> To share (*knowledgeably*)

close enough

> To explain (*additionally*)

to what ails mankind!

> To state (*realizingly*)

It was a child's way of seeing things—

> To dismiss (*curtly*)

or

> To dramatize (*knowlingly*)

an idealist's.

> To wrap up (*conclusively*)

Peter

Peter arrives at the Chicago Art Institute in a state of pique. He travels from acerbic annoyance to demandingly expressing his truth. Along his trajectory he expresses love, pain, truth, condescension, warmth, understanding, defiance, awareness, frustration, insecurity, and alarm. Recall when a best friend caused you frustration tempered with caring and love, causing you to reveal new and vulnerable truths.

What a perky Seventies kind of gal you are!

> To define (*wryly*)

You can separate sexual needs

> To inform (*ironically*)

from emotional dependencies.

> To declare (*emphatically*)

Heidi,

> To get her attention (*quizzically*)

if you tell me you secrete endorphins when you run,

> To confront (*realistically*)

I'm going straight into the curator's office

    To inform (*threateningly*)

and demand an all armor retrospective.

    To define (*intentionally*)

Actually,

    To level (*openly*)

I'm afraid I'm feeling sort of distant from you.

    To inform (*honestly*)

I'm not criticizing you.

    To clarify (*carefully*)

It's just how I'm feeling.

    To explain (*truthfully*)

I haven't seen you in eight months.

    To inform (*specifically*)

Heidi,

    To waken (*alertingly*)

I don't play on your team.

    To inform (*simply*)

I've become a liberal homosexual pediatrician.

    To declare (*openly*)

And

    To add (*mysteriously*)

I prefer Stanley.

    To inform (*defiantly*)

My friend's name is Stanley Zinc.

    To include (*lovingly*)

He's a child psychiatrist from Johns Hopkins.

    To impress (*proudly*)

But

    To grab her interest (*playfully*)

he's thinking of quitting

    To share (*informingly*)

in order to study with Merce Cunningham.

    To divert (*knowingly*)

The sad thing is

    To inform (*lovingly*)

that Stanley is too old

    To state (*factually*)

to join the company

    To inform (*honestly*)

and

    To further (*conspiratorily*)

Miss Merce isn't getting any younger, either.

    To amuse (*facetiously*)

Anyway,

    To change the subject (*upliftingly*)

I'm thinking of replacing him

    To pique her interest (*temptingly*)

with a waiter I met last week,

    To inform (*revealingly*)

we share a mutual distrust of Laura Nyro.

    To inform (*unitedly*)

I would have told you all this earlier

    To inform (*sharingly*)

but

    To control (*attentively*)

I thought we deserved something more intimate

    To explain (*truthfully*)

than a phone call.

    To share (*sarcastically*)

So

    To inform (*cutely*)

I chose the Chicago Art Institute.

    To amuse (*snidely*)

Heidi,

    To get her attention (*impatiently*)

I'm gay,

    To reveal (*truthfully*)

okay?

    To ask (*clearly*)

I sleep with Stanley Zinc, M.D.

    To inform (*repeatedly*)

And my *liberation,*

    To define (*personally*)

my *pursuit of happiness,*

    To specify (*additionally*)

and *the pursuit of happiness of other men like me*

    To inform (*declaritively*)

is just as politically

    to explain (*meaningfully*)

and socially

    To add (*spontaneously*)

valid

    to declare (*emphatically*)

as hanging a couple of Goddamned paintings

    To compare (*shallowly*)

because they were signed by someone named Nancy,

    To specify (*condescendingly*)

Gladys,

    To add (*uncontrollably*)

or Gilda.

To press the point (*humorously*)

And

To hold her attention (*emphatically*)

that is why I came to see you today.

To inform (*truthfully*)

I am demanding your equal time

To express (*demandingly*)

and consideration.

To close (*completely*)

Proving Your Character's Justification

You are now familiar with your character, aware of what makes her tick. You have chosen her objective and decided upon actions for creating her inner life and emotional journey. Adding adjustments developed her behavior and persona. Still, you have unanswered questions about her.

Rereading the text will uncover facts you may have overlooked. Your knowledge of the character was more general when you read it earlier. Certain information and events did not have importance for you. Now you see dialogue and events anew, shedding light and opening doors of understanding. Your new knowledge helps prove your character's justification for his choices and actions.

Justification is exactly what it sounds like. There are reasons, arguments, or discussions substantiating every action and word. If someone takes an action against you, retaliation in some form may be justified. Justification puts your character in the driver's seat, making him active and allowing him to believe he is doing the right thing. It gives your character permission to behave, physically and emotionally, as he deems correct for himself. Your character's behavior is justified by the facts, truth, and detail you find in rereading the text.

Proving justification for your character's behavior supports the validity of your choices. The stronger you believe in your choices, the deeper commitment you bring to each moment. The more committed, the more believable your character. Justifying your character underscores, with assurance, your knowledge of the truth in your character's behavior.

Edmund

In rereading *King Lear*, you find a greater importance in his final line.

> *Yet Edmund was beloved.*

Edmund's last thought before dying justifies choosing the objective of needing his father's love and acceptance. Gloucester's partiality to Edgar justifies Edmund's calling on Nature. She is impartial and in Nature's realm mankind is created equal.

> *Who, in the lusty stealth of nature, take*
> *more composition and fierce quality*
> *Than doth, within a dull, stale, tired bed,*
> *Go to th' creating a whole tribe of fops*
> *Got 'tween asleep and wake?*

This justifies his belief about deserving to inherit his father's title and estate.

Edmund's actions stem from the need everyone shares, that of love and acceptance from parents.

Serafina

Serafina's life was built around Rosario. She was Rosario's wife and Rosa's mother. She had no identity of her own. His death left her unsure of who she is or what her life will be. She builds a shell around herself, refusing to acknowledge even the most apparent signs he may have been unfaithful. She is justified in her feelings of what Rosario has done for her. A peasant girl from Sicily who married a landowner and was brought to America, she was offered a new life by Rosario.

Needing to hold onto her dreams and beliefs, she chooses to live by pushing away the truth and creating a life of denial. She has already been emotionally shattered. Clinging to his ashes symbolizes her desire to live in the past with him. The depth of her passion and sexual feelings along with the need to have a man in her life justifies the objective of wanting to have her shell penetrated.

Serafina is a contradiction. Finding her core takes careful scrutiny to justify her actions and behavior. She is a complex woman unaware of her own complexity.

Beneatha

Beneatha expresses herself through humor, brashness, and out-spokenness. She delights in shocking her family with irreverence, superiority, and defiance. She appears to be ambitious, directed, overachieving, and forthright.

Reread the text, and discover the subtle ways her dreams are minimized by members of her family, justifying her motivation to rise above their wishes. Many of her actions are justifiably rebellious. Her thinking is progressive. Her desire to be a doctor goes far beyond the simple hopes and dreams the Youngers live with. She believes in experiencing the American dream available to all Americans in its truest form. Beneatha's major justification for her behavior is her youth. She is twenty years old and precocious. She has always been precocious, and probably when she was a child, everyone thought it was charming and funny.

She has a contradictory nature justified by both her rebellious nature and her respect for her mother. She is a woman of extremes—speaking out against assimilation yet straightening her hair. Wearing the African robes yet changing out of them at George's request. Decrying God and obeying her mother.

The purity of her desire is profound and justifies her dream of becoming a doctor. The effect of Walter Lee's actions clearly justifies her feeling of nothingness.

Peter

As a graduate of Williams College, a good liberal arts college, there is justification for Peter's use of literary and musical references in his dialogue. Enriching his life with literature and music is important to him.

Peter reveals deeply personal aspects about himself in a less than intimate setting because of his insight into Heidi's emotional emptiness and his need to reach her at all costs. His need to help her see what she is doing to her life justifies his behavior.

Peter is justified in his seeming harshness in trying to reach Heidi. She doesn't hear him. Peter's love for Heidi justifies his feelings in the moment. He wants her to understand the important role she plays in his life, justifying his demand for equal reciprocity.

Reread the text. The final scene justifies the insights Peter has about Heidi. Here you discover the depth of Peter's insightfulness. His concern for Heidi in his monologue is proven at this moment.

Proving your character's justification allows you to fully commit and believe in the truth of your character. It offfers you spontaneity and the freedom to play each moment and action to its fullest.

Exploring for Opposites

Opposites play against the text. Using opposites surprises an audience and creates mystery and danger, allowing the character to behave unexpectedly. Comedy needs emotional investment. Drama or tragedy needs an honest organic infusion of comedy. These are opposites you can bring to the moment. In a comedy, find the character's life-and-death importance. In drama, look for moments of honest humor, allowing the audience to breath and take in the emotion-filled moments.

In comedy, the humor often comes from the situation and/or circumstance surrounding your character. The audience finds it funny, but your character takes it seriously.

Think of a time you were about to leave your home for an audition or appointment and couldn't find your keys. You begin by looking in the usual places. As the minutes tick away, you become more agitated and frustrated at the thought of being late. You begin looking slowly and methodically. In no time, your search frantically accelerates. You begin overturning items, tossing things around. Anxiety builds. Finally coming to a standstill, you burst into tears. You put your hand in your pocket and voila! It was not funny to you, but it would appear quite funny to someone watching. It's funny because in the moment it was of life-and-death importance to you.

A sad or dramatic situation needs to be lightened to get through those moments. People survive by finding the lightness in the dark. Opposites prevent your character from wallowing in self-pity. Using opposites allows both sides to coexist in the moment.

Edmund

Edmund calls upon Nature to help him make a decision, a decision that could have a profound effect on all of Britain. Suddenly, he chooses to lighten things up by talking about the inconsequential differences between him and his brother.

> *...my dimensions are as well compact, my mind as generous, and my shape as true....*

The argument he chooses to offer Nature is of opposite weight to his plan, omitting any discussion of morality, integrity, or even depth of character.

Serafina

Serafina knows she is looked down on by Flora and Bessie. They see her as sad and lost. Instead, she offers them triumph.

> *...I'm satisfied to remember, because I had the best.*

She brings the opposite to the story of her loss of love. Serafina does not wallow; she soars.

> *Not the third best and not the second best, but the first best, the only best!*

She is not just the winner, but the champ. She is emphatic. This is not the tone of a romantic, intimate story. It is a description of winning.

> *I know what love-making was. And I'm satisfied just to remember.*

The truth of what is in her soul is the opposite of what she is saying. She is trapped in her denial, looking for someone to penetrate her barriers and free her. Her words and actions belie her emotional, spiritual, and physical needs.

Beneatha

Beneatha answers Asagai's question with a question.

> *Me?*

She is devastated and lost. She questions Asagai's question.

> *Me?*

The second one-word question asks Asagai why he wants to know. She hopes he has an answer for her. She begins to see the absurdity of her situation.

> *Me, I'm nothing.*

Again, Beneatha gives a brief response, this time not questioning. Her newfound self is defiant and strong in her nothingness. She communicates Beneatha may be down but not out for the count.

> *Me.*

Her next response is definitive. Having just heard her describe herself as nothing, she is amused by this revelation. She knows better than to believe what she has just said, bringing irony to the moment.

Using opposites in these few brief phrases, Beneatha presents a complex person experiencing herself for the first time. Opposites create a moment, not of nothingness, but of color, life, truth, and profound awareness.

Peter

Peter left a busy schedule at the hospital and rushed to Heidi, only to discover she merely needed his body to count at her feminist rally. He is furious and uses opposites to get her attention.

What a perky Seventies kind of gal you are!

He opts for irony that both diverts Heidi and ameliorates his fury.

You can separate sexual needs from emotional dependencies.

The thought of Heidi going through life compartmentalized and devoid of emotional connection horrifies Peter. He uses an opposite tact to get Heidi to believe he is proud of her, hoping she will hear his truth. Peter whimsically tells her she is turning into a man.

Peter's use of opposites displays his intelligence and concern. Concern shown through the depth of his anger and his need to set her straight.

Opposites create complexity within the character, allowing the audience to discover through surprises, mystery, and humor the true meaning of what they are communicating. Opposites demand attention because they create the unexpected.

Finding the Humor

Funerals can be funny. Weddings sad. Humor comes in many ways, and often when least expected. Humor helps humans through dire situations. It is an important survival instinct, creating self-awareness and relief from the absurdity of life. Using humor often breaks the ice, opening a door to conversation. People often laugh at themselves. Self-deprecation can be charming and make a character vulnerable, bringing an audience to her side. It can be used as shared recognition. A sort of "Ah, yes I can relate to that. I recognize it." Humor invested in sad moments often adds surprise and an unexpected depth. Look for humor in your character's life, but use it only when it is organic and truthful.

Jokes are not humor. Many characters knowingly tell jokes. Don't shy away from these moments. The character expects a laugh; if it doesn't come, allow him to acknowledge the lameness of his joke. His reaction can be humourous and display self-knowledge, endearing him to the other person and the audience.

Humor protects your character from feeling sorry for himself, preventing him from becoming self-pitying. By communicating pain through humor, the audience is surprised into feeling for your character.

All characters fight life and death struggles. This profound seriousness can be leavened with humor, creating a life force revealing strength. Humor adds perseverance, endurance, subtlety, and complexity.

Edmund

Edmund uses humor to express the absurdity of his situation.

> *Why brand they us with base?*
> *with baseness? bastardy? base, base?*

The absurdity of his birth does not escape him. He is aware of the incredulousness of the effect of his father's dalliance, allowing him to incorporate and share his wry humor with Nature.

Using humor, Edmund adds an element of surprise by bringing a lighter side to his destructive plan. Nature is not asked to feel Edmund's pain but to share his humor at the absurdity of his situation.

Using humor charms Nature into accepting a plan of devastation. Edmund's clever use of humor lightens the seriousness, unexpectedly catching the audience and portraying himself as a strong and knowing person.

Serafina

Serafina is an uneducated woman possessing common sense. She trusts her instinct about life and people. Her speech, which might be sentimental and maudlin, has humor, thus making it triumphant and insightful. She humorously expresses her reason for holding onto Rosario rather than looking for a new man.

> *...I went to some other, some middle-aged man,*
> *not young, not full of young passion, but getting a*
> *pot belly on him and losing his hair and smelling*
> *of sweat and liquor....*

This description explains humorously her decision to cling to her memories. In Serafina's case, humor adds a dimension of sadness.

Her use of humor displays an indomitable personality under-scored with vulnerability, along with a powerful sexual nature and drive. Using humor, she continues sharing with Flora and Bessie the ridiculousness of their trip to New Orleans.

> *Go on, you do it, you go on the streets and let them*
> *drop their sacks of dirty water on you!*

Her advice is encouragement tinged with irony.

Her humor is self-protective. She doesn't wallow in her feelings but keeps them at arm's length by offering the two women the beauty of true love.

Beneatha

Beneatha uses acerbic and biting humor to demonstrate her self-awareness. It aids her in opening to the truth of her present situation. Her situation may have changed but Beneatha has not.

> *Me? ... Me? ... Me, I'm nothing ... Me.*

She struggles to maintain her humor. Her irony allows her to survive a dark moment that appears to have taken over her life.

Peter

Peter expresses himself with intelligent, perceptive, and cunning humor throughout the play. His feelings toward Heidi make him want to lash out at her. In his very personal style, he does it with wry humor.

> *What a perky Seventies kind of gal you are!*

This ironic description displays Peter's intelligence and the insightfulness of his perception of an emotionally damaged Heidi. Displaying his quick wit and style, he informs her that he has heard her and that he feels for the misguided direction of her life.

> *Heidi, if you tell me you secrete endorphins when*
> *you run, I'm going straight into the curator's office*
> *and demand an all armor retrospective.*

Peter uses biting humor to charm Heidi into hearing the seriousness of his message. He is not judging her. He cares. He uses humor to open her. Heidi's situation is serious, and Peter knows her well enough to realize the humorous path is the way to reach her.

The variety of ways these characters use humor in important moments helps the other person to hear and receive the full seriousness of each situation. Humor keeps the focus on the issue by diverting the other person into listening.

Personalizing Your Character

Personalizing your character brings her to life. It calls for your emotional investment. Personalization expresses honestly your character's experiences and the emotional truth in each moment. It requires your total involvement in every moment. Bringing your personal experience and emotional truth to your character's life allows blood to flow through her veins, creating recognizable life. These moments need to be alive in the moment and experienced for the first time. Personalizing her life infuses her with true emotional color.

Personalization uses your responses, sensorily and emotionally, to enrich your character. Awareness of how you specifically react to hot weather, early morning, aromas, colors, and different clothing aids you in bringing these personalizations to your work. Knowledge of your personal honesty and truth allows you to commit fully to your character's emotional life. Investigate the character's emotional moments, and find a comparable one in your own life when you experienced a similar emotion. Explore these moments in detail. Each of these details needs to be personally invested in and committed to your character's inner life.

What you need to explore are comparable emotional experiences. It is no help to look for a comparable situation or circumstance. Look for the moments you walked a similar emotional path.

Edmund

Edmund calls upon Nature. Define Nature for yourself. Is it God? Is it Mother Nature? Explore your sensations and feelings in the moments you ask for help. This is a comparable sensory and emotional moment you want to personalize.

Finding your specific higher power needs to be explored for your own truth and honesty. If your believe in God, it will be easy to explore the moments you have reached out for God's guidance. If you don't believe in a God, explore your own perception of a universal being you believe in. The universe was created with such perfection, it is hard to believe it is man's handiwork. Whatever super being you have reached out to needs to be explored for the complexity of emotions you experience in those moments.

Edmund's pain stems from his illegitimate birth. This may not resonate for you. Find a moment when you experienced being treated as an outcast. Explore your emotional pain in minute detail and invest Edmund's profoundly felt need with your specific emotional truth. Look for moments when you were denied acceptance. Define the person from whom you needed acceptance. Maybe yours was not a parent but an acting teacher or a mentor who never offered approval. This is a comparable emotional experience you can commit to Edmund's need.

Relive these emotional truths in the moment for the first time. Your awareness of these reawakened personal feelings brings Edmund alive in the moment

Edmund's feeling of competition toward Edgar also needs your personal responses to create the depth of insecurity Edmund experiences in his soul. Find a person in your life who makes you feel second class, a person whose very presence brings out your insecurity. Bring this person to Edmund's speech.

Edmund's world created with your personalization makes him your original conception.

Serafina

Your personal feelings of intense and powerful love need to be instilled in Serafina to believe in her defiant desire to remain in the past. Her relationship with Rosario, once filled with joy and satisfaction, has been replaced with sadness and loss. The facts of your relationship may not be the same but you will have experienced the depth of emotions. If you have not yet had a profound love, explore your experience of unconditional love. It may be with a pet. The feelings you experienced are real. Infuse Serafina with your truth and personal feelings to realize the depth of her love. Don't look for the right person but for similar honest and truthful feelings. The experience of loving makes Serafina cared for, recognizable, and understood.

Another element that needs to be fulfilled is Serafina's profound sense of loss. Find your own powerful loss, dredge up the sadness of your feelings. Feel them in every moment, with every pore of your being. Bring this immediacy to Serafina.

Personalizing Serafina's sexual satisfaction is of paramount importance. Look for, experience, and define these feelings in yourself. Serafina's passion makes her alive. Find this sexual truth in your body. Bring to her the moments your body felt alive and tingled with raw sexual energy.

Serafina's disheveled appearance needs your exploration. Find precise aspects in your emotional life that impel you to refuse to care about your physical appearance.

Beneatha

Beneatha is emotionally bereft at the top of her monologue. Truthfully revealing this numbness is scary for her. Finding this personal and emotional truth in your life's experience will make it real. Peel away your layers. Bring yourself to this feeling of nothingness, making Benetha live with your personal feelings of devastation. Your devastation may have occurred when you lost the role you desired with all your heart and you believed it was all over for you. Examine in detail how you fought to lift yourself from these feelings. Bring the truth of your experience to Beneatha's reality to connect with her pain and numbness. This depth of feeling is what you want to communicate and share.

Peter

Peter's disappointment in Heidi makes him feel abandoned, misused, and abused. She has placed their friendship on the back burner of her life.

Explore moments of great disappointment caused by an important person in your life. This is a much needed personal moment to explore. Peter needs to be filled with your emotional truth, propelling him to attack and share his truth with Heidi. Dredge up a time you were disappointed and conflicted yet needed to be truthful with someone you care about. Awaken the difficulties you experienced and magnify them a hundred times. This is the level of difficulty Peter experiences when revealing himself. Don't make it easy for him.

Explore the reasons it was difficult. Commit them to Peter's immediate life. Your personalizaton brings honesty and reality to his need. The more personal detail and specificity you invest in him, the more universal he becomes.

Peter is wearing jeans. Explore his feelings about himself in jeans. Is he is as comfortable in jeans as he is in his doctor's scrubs and coat? Does he feel as strong an identity in jeans as he does when he appears as Dr. Patrone. After exploring your personal feelings relating to clothes, you will be able to bring your personal truth to Peter in this moment.

Your work needs personal investment to fully bring your character to life. Involving your own personal experiences allows you to believe in your character's truth. Personalize every detail and moment of your work.

As you read and reread the text, explore each moment that grabs your consciousness. These are instinctively the moments to bring to your character. Try not to intellectualize these instinctual feelings. Jot them down so you can go back and examine them when you begin your personalization process.

Trust your instinct. It will guide you to the correct personal choices in making your character yours. Personalization brings truth and honesty to your character as he travels his emotional journey.

Personal emotional experiences are inherent in all human beings and makes them universal, recognizable, and understood. These personal truths create the contradictions in your character that are shared with all humans.

Utilizing Research

Utilizing research about your character adds dimension and truth. Research brings a rich and full history to draw upon throughout your monologue. It aids in creating specificity by bringing personal knowledge and comprehensive reasons for making his most important decisions. The text contains necessary information but often does not go into detail about the social climate, political atmosphere, or other outside pressures brought to bear on your character's life. Popular culture of the day adds to his emotional makeup. The text places your character in a particular city or country about which you may have only generalized or limited knowledge. Detailed information of the place helps clarify moments, adding to the larger picture of the outside world and its effect on your character.

Today Americans live with the effects of 9/11 and the threat of terrorism. Living at such a time and experiencing its stressful effects on your life can help you understand how research can enrich your character. Each period has its own political and social turmoil. Take nothing for granted. Learn about specific incidents caused by the political and social climate of the time and its effects on your character.

Religion is an area where research adds interest and truth. If your character has been raised with certain religious beliefs, the effects may add to her inner conflict. Learn the tenets of the specific religion, and decipher how it affects your character's choices.

Your character's education is an important area requiring research. Consider the amount and quality of the education along with knowledge of their schools. Each school and university has its own environment and provides additional information for you to include in the life of your character.

Researching each aspect of your character's life enhances the knowledge you bring to each moment. The text may not explore any of the social, political, or religious aspects of your character, but the external pressures affect him. Effects come overtly from newspapers, magazines, radio, and television and subliminally through music, books, and movies.

Research brings additional complexity to your character by contributing to the depth of his feelings about important choices he needs to make. It also adds information to help in deciding on his specific objective.

Edmund

Edmund lives in the eighth century BC. Conditions were primitive and barbaric. Life was lived with physical hardships. Castles were built of stone and were always drafty and cold. The only warmth was from fire. Animals were hunted and killed for food. Clothing was rough and heavy, made of coarsely woven heavy fabrics or the furs from the slain animals. Travel was slow and limited to horses or horse-drawn wagons and coaches. These limitations made the world a very small place for most people. News traveled slowly.

Men carried swords. Violence and death were solutions to many personal and political problems. Women were in the backseat. Those who inherited empires, as Regan and Goneril do, handed power to their husbands and had control through manipulation.

It was a time of strict protocol and formality. Children addressed their parents formally and were treated as property. Class was defined by titles and adhered to by members of the family as well as outsiders and servants. Everyone knew her or his place and standing in the community.

In this pre-Christian period, Nature was treated as a godlike power, all-knowing, impartial, and nonjudgmental. It was a fair and equalizing force in helping make decisions and shedding light on difficult situations. Many of the characters in the play call upon Nature during times of strife.

The eighth century BC is a time foreign to us. Researching it aids you in creating the specifics of life at this time. Find readings or viewing materials about the period. Research gives insight and information into lifestyle, behavior, relationships, and protocol.

Serafina

Serafina was born in Sicily. Researching Sicily's topography and location at the southern heel of Italy's boot offers specific knowledge of Serafina's ability to deal with the climate on the coast of Louisiana. Travel was much less advanced. Serafina and Rosario probably came to America by freighter. During the long trip, they must have experienced both joy at the prospect of coming to America and hardships during the crossing.

Serafina was raised in the 1930s. What was life like for a peasant girl in the 1930s? Has the move to Louisiana offered her more privileges? Research the politics of the time. War was looming large throughout Europe. This may have been a motivating force in Rosario's decision to move them to America. Franklin Roosevelt was the president, and it was a time of great hope in the United States. There was much emigration to the United States with hopes created by the American dream.

It was also a time of limited and slower forms of communication. There was no television to educate and inform Serafina of world events and changes. News traveled more slowly. When she wrote to her family, she probably only received mail back from them after a long time. The telephone is new to her, and long distance calls were expensive. She displays her frugality and her unwillingness to use the telephone when Alvaro wants to make a phone call. Her feelings toward the telephone also point out her desire to remain in the past and not move into the present.

The possibility of prosperity was a highly held dream. America was barely emerging from the Depression. Times were hard, and money scarce. That may have been a factor in Serafina's decision to refine her sewing skills and bring in additional income, especially after Rosa's birth.

Beneatha

Beneatha lives on the South Side of Chicago in the 1950s. The South Side is one of the poorer sections of Chicago. This speaks to the economic standing of the Younger family and identifies the importance of the money from Beneatha's father's insurance.

Eisenhower was president, and the effects of the Cold War loomed large in American households. The country was still recovering from the effects of the Second World War. The economy was picking up, but times were still tough in African-American communities. The Civil Rights movement had not yet occurred, and "Negro" was still the preferred word.

Many homes had television, but not the Younger's. Research into the economic constraints on African Americans explains Beneatha's aggressive drive and determination to better her situation.

The information and insight Beneatha gets from the politics of the rising Civil Rights movement support her dreams of upward mobility and equality for women. Understanding where women and African Americans stood in the educational and cultural communities brings importance and daring to Beneatha's life choices.

College was a rarity for African Americans then, medical school even more daring. Specific knowledge gained through research adds to the external pressure forcing Beneatha to behave in a protected and cynical manner.

Peter

Peter was born in the late 1940s and spent his formative years in the 1950's. He was raised on Chicago's North Side. The North Side is the upper middle class section of Chicago. The Patrones are most likely wealthy, educated, and informed. They give Peter the best of everything.

Knowing he went to St. Mark's Academy, a Catholic school, gives us insight into his strict Catholic upbringing and explains the formal look he presents when the audience first meets him. His arrival at the Chicago Institute of Art wearing jeans and carrying a backpack makes clear his life changes.

When he first approaches Heidi, he refers to himself as a small noise from Winnetka. An odd phrase. Does he come from Winnetka? Is Winnetka on Chicago's North Side? No explanation is given. In order to give this moment its full meaning, research is needed. The research reveals Peter's play on words. He is referring to the hit song "Big Noise from Winnetka" by Gene Krupa, a major star of the big band era. This not only makes clear Peter's attachment to popular music, which he mentions throughout but also informs of his self-image. Calling himself "a small noise from Winnetka" gives insight into his feelings about himself.

Another interesting moment revealed in Peter and Heidi's first meeting is the sanatorium scenario Peter plays and Heidi picks up on. It is a game, but it is based on literary references from Thomas Mann. Give these moments their full value and they will offer specific insights into Peter's background. These two moments speak of a childhood spent reading and listening to music.

Peter tells Heidi he is about to enter Williams College. This is an important fact. Researching Williams College, you will find it is an important liberal arts college. Stephen Sondheim is a famous alumni. Literature, music, and languages are major courses of study. Peter uses literary and musical references throughout the play, along with a smattering of French phrases. Researching his education aids in understanding its importance to him and brings truth and firsthand knowledge.

In his monologue, he talks about Merce Cunningham. He speaks with knowledge of this well-known modern dance choreographer. Research him, his dance company, and his particular style. The same holds true for Laura Nyro. Listen to her music, and understand her lyrics. This helps you in making an informed choice about the "mutual distrust" he and the waiter share. Laura Nyro's lyrics had political, social, and emotional content making them something to embrace or distrust. Again, research informs your choice by bringing additional specificity to these moments.

Research brings specificity and detailed variety. Research educates. Read, listen to music, look at magazines to discover facts and knowledge from different periods. Watch films. Look at clothes. Talk to your parents and grandparents. Learn what life was like before television, before news was heard every half hour. Understand the rhythms of life in a slower time, people's behavior before the jet age, and how this insularity affected people. Historical periods are different and add subtle nuances and texture to your character's being.

Research enriches moments. When you come across phrases appearing to be more than they seem, check into them. Research yields rich rewards.

Enriching with Your Senses

Enriching with your senses involves you fully in each moment. Life is a sensory experience. Each moment of every day one of your senses affects you. Acting needs to include your senses. Involving your sensory awareness brings your character into the moment.

Groggily awake in the morning, somnambulistically stumbling toward the kitchen, you smell freshly brewed coffee snapping you alert and bringing you into the moment. Your olfactory sense changes your state of being. This is how your senses create truth.

Your head is filled with thoughts about an audition you have just had. You are consumed with dissecting every moment. You are totally wrapped up in your thoughts. Suddenly, a flash of red breaks in attracting your vision. It's red hair belonging to an attractive woman. Your visual sense brings you into the present. You smile and delight in the vision. It passes, and you go back to assessing your audition. Your senses are always affected. They bring you into the moment. Invest your character with sensory awareness to create moment-to-moment truth.

Sensory experiences are personal. They are your secret. These sensory sensations enrich and deepen the fabric of your character. They reveal your character's truth. They add detail. Your senses ground you, bringing you into the present. A sensory experience can only be had in the moment. You can only smell, hear, touch, taste, or see in the moment. You can talk about what you have seen but can only see in the moment. Using your senses brings immediacy to your character's life.

Everyone tastes, smells, sees, hears, and feels in the same way. Become aware of your particular sensory experiences. Bring these specifics to your work. Explore each sense. Standing in a florist's shop watching someone smell a hyacinth plant, you immediately connect with the look of sensual pleasure that comes over him. It is much easier than communicating an idea or thought and can be done without words. Incorporate this awareness into your character's life, and experience a heightened emotional commitment.

Edmund

Edmund is alone and convening with Nature. Is it warm or cold? Sunny or gray? Morning or evening? Visit a private place in a park or atop a hill. Go at several different times of the day, in different weather. There are trees and sounds all around. There may be a breeze or stillness. Experience the sensory differences. One will be right for you to invest in Edmund's moment with Nature.

See and feel nature around you. Experience the universe in all its glories—the greenery, the trees, the natural sounds. Bring this to Edmund's speech. He doesn't have to look up to experience nature. Nature surrounds him, infiltrating his eyes, nose, and ears; even the air feels different on different parts of his exposed skin. Each sensory element keeps him alive in the moment. Nature is his partner, the other person. Take the speech indoors, and you will miss Nature's involvement with him.

Edmund holds a letter in his hand. Probably made of parchment. Heavier than paper. This letter may change his life. It feels all-powerful in his hand. It may change the future of Britain. Edmund experiences the weight in his hand. It burns with intensity.

Personalizing this letter and making it sensorily alive creates its weight and importance. It is not merely a piece of paper, but the key to Edmund's future life.

Serafina

The Gulf Coast of Louisiana is hot, muggy, and always moist. The month is June when most graduations take place. It is not yet the dog days of August, but it is still warm and muggy. Explore how Serafina deals with heat and humidity. Is her rhythm affected? Explore how heat affects you. Live with the sensations of a muggy and moist day. Invest Serafina with this sensory truth.

When telling Flora and Bessie of her love for Rosario, she expresses the sensual experience of holding him close and feeling his skin. Invest Serafina with the sensual aliveness his skin creates on her body. She is a sensual woman possessing a heightened sense of her sensuality. Each moment of her speech needs to be infused with specific and truthful sensual sensation.

Every sensation she shares with Flora and Bessie needs to be explored. Each must be fully experienced, personalized, and committed to Serafina who wants to pierce through the hides of the two women. This honest and truthful sensuality is of paramount importance in creating Serafina.

She has spent many nights with tears running down her face. Feel the tears. Relive the path they take down your face and how they feel on each part of your skin as they roll down. She talks about the dampness on the pillow. Experience this clammy sensation for yourself in order to be able to offer the truth.

Recall your specific sensual experiences during sex. There is no faking the orgasm Serafina relives. She sensorily relives each and every moment truthfully, honestly, lovingly, and proudly. Explore an orgasm of total satisfaction. This sensation needs to be honestly embedded in Serafina to relate her powerful need to keep Rosario in her life. She relives feeling his skin, the pleasure he brought her, his smell, touch, and sounds, and the pounding of his body on hers. A pleasure like no other in life. This is what she is holding onto. This is what she is unwilling to release from her grasp.

Working on the blouse for Flora, Serafina experiences the fabric in her hands. The polka dots on the fabric. Know the specific feeling of the fabric. Explore the difference between silk, cotton, and polyester. Allow Serafina to experience the fabric in the moment, bringing her heightened sense into play as she works on the blouse.

Beneatha

Beneatha begins to tell the story of Rufus as if for the first time. She is experiencing the cold and blinding whiteness of the snow. Bring it along with you. The stronger she creates the cold, the more it will envelope and allow Asagai to comprehend the effect it had on her. Make Asagai chilly by incorporating your sensation of the cold. Know how cold effects you. Does it exhilarate or chill you? Feel the cold on your nose. See the blinding white of freshly fallen snow.

Put yourself on the sled going down that hill. The world flashing by. Feeling your body out of your control. These images heighten your senses, making them alive at every moment. If you have never been on a sled zooming down a hill, recall a roller coaster ride and the sensation of your stomach rising into your mouth as you drop down that first deep dip. Experience the mixture of exhilaration and fear that exist hand in hand.

This is what needs to be invested sensorily in the sledding moments as Beneatha describes them. The deeper she draws him into the whiteness of the snow, experiencing the exciting and enjoyable ride on the sled, the greater the shock when the red blood is added to the picture. The red of Rufus's blood destroying the whiteness of the snow. The shock of his blood hits her as powerfully now as it did the first time all those many years ago.

See the blood. The exact shade of red. See it on the stark white of the snow. Reawaken how you feel when you see blood. Bring it to the moment, allowing it to upset the entire picture. Allow Beneatha to involve Asagai's visual sense. Get him to see new blood gushing from a wound. The sight of his face split open is imprinted on her memory. It has never left her nor will it. If you have ever been involved in an accident or observed one, the image can be brought back immediately. A wounded body imprints itself on your sensory being.

Explore and accept the truth of these sensory sensations. Allow them to come careening at you, tumbling at you one after another, overwhelming you. This is the experience Beneatha is having as she relates the story of how she found her calling to the medical profession.

As if all this wasn't enough, add the loud, intruding, screeching sound of the ambulance's siren. The sound is earsplitting. Take that sound and magnify it. Make it hurt your eardrums. Force yourself to sensorily respond to this imposing sound that adds to the chaos of speed, snow, and laughter shattered by Rufus' accident.

Investing Beneatha with sensory truth forces Asagai to live the accident with her.

Peter

Peter is in the vast openness of the Chicago Art Institute. It is hard to hear. Heidi is distracted. Peter has to work hard to get and keep her attention. Relive a moment in a parking lot or on a bridge where the openness created its own sounds and forced you to raise your voice to be heard. Realize the difficulty of keeping your focus. Peter fights to quiet his senses. In this instance, his sensory awareness needs to be quieted down. He says intimate things in a vast openness, trying to speak loudly yet privately.

Peter's backpack has weight. His difficulty reaching Heidi makes him aware of its weight, which is adding to his difficulties. His body adjusts. Add these sensory feelings to an already uncomfortable situation. This discomfort brings additional truth and grounds Peter in the moment.

Peter mentions meeting a waiter in a restaurant. Talking about the waiter recalls the restaurant. Together they create the scenario. Know what attracted Peter. Eyes? Hair? Smile? Choose someone you are attracted to, someone you have only seen but not spoken with. Know what it is that attracts you. Flash this image before you. Attraction heightens the sensory experience.

Select a restaurant you know. Recall its color scheme, its size and arrangement of tables and booths. Pick a familiar restaurant and specifically bring your senses into play. Go back to the restaurant and have a meal. Relive your sensory experiences: the smells, the sounds, the sight of waiters moving around with plates of food. Bring these detailed sensory images to the truth of the moment. This is where Peter was sensually and sexually awakened to the waiter. The sensory feelings you experience express Peter's truth in the moment.

Explore each sensory facet of your monologue. These elements are important. They fulfill the truth and reality of your character's moment-to-moment reality. People experience life through their senses. Become aware of them. Add them to your work for variety and depth. Your senses make moments real and alive. The details you experience in sensory moments communicate the truth of your character. Your senses ground you, bringing specificity to the truth of the moment. They bring you into the present, making your character richer and more recognizable to your audience.

7

Inhabiting Your Character and Fulfilling Their Needs

Choosing an objective has given your character a raison d'etre and an emotional journey. You have built your character's skeletal foundation. Now add flesh to that skeleton by inhabiting his or her heart and soul.

Up to this point, you have been objectively working your actor's tools, which your character is unaware of. Inhabiting your character begins the subjective work of experiencing your character from the "I" perspective. Your choices will now be subjective, experienced from the character's needs. Fulfilling your character's needs creates a fully realized, three-dimensional person.

Knowing Your Character's Past (History)

Everyone has a history, a history of facts, eventful moments, and psychological results from childhood, school days, adolescence, teen years, early dating, and college days. Everyone has effects from relationships with other people: family, friends, lovers, and teachers. Everyone has likes and dislikes: food, books, movies, music, and climatic conditions. Everyone has birthdays, both enjoyed and best forgotten. Know your character's history as you know your own.

Develop your character's past from birth. His behavior patterns take shape during these early years through interactions with siblings, playmates, and adults. This information begins the subjective process of inhabiting your character.

All you know about yourself is needed for your character. Asked when your birthday is, your response is immediate. It is knowledge embedded in your psyche. If asked about your favorite food, you might take a moment to choose from many, but you instinctively have choices. Questions asked of your past are answered with specific knowledge. Events in your life created your emotional makeup, behavior, and psychology. These aspects help create your character with its specific likes, dislikes, aesthetics, values, and morals.

The author creates your character's present. Developing her precise history allows your character to spontaneously soar into her present situation and circumstance, ready to take her emotional journey toward achieving her objective.

Answer the following questions from the "I" perspective: When was I born? Where was I born? What kind of childhood did I have? How did I feel about my mother and father? How do I feel about them now? How do I feel about my siblings? How do you feel about not having any siblings? How much schooling have I had? What are my religious beliefs? Political affiliations?

Familiarity with your character enables you to answer these questions. Look for clues in the text. Treat it like the bible of your character. It is a font of knowledge. With familiarity comes new awareness of the clues. Actions can be changed to be more specific as your character develops. Your character's past is second nature.

Edmund

Edmund was born in the eighth century BC. He says he is:

> . . . *some twelve or fourteen moonshines lag of a brother . . .*

specifying the proximity of their births. Edgar's legitimacy places him in line to be the sole heir of his father's title and estate. Edmund's illegitimacy has caused him major psychological and emotional damage. His feelings of being an outcast are painful, prompting him to take drastic actions to overcome this stigma.

Edmund has been away for nine years, half of his life. This exile has caused Edmund to experience alienation and isolation from his father and brother, creating the deeper wounds of feeling unloved and unaccepted.

If this exile had been a happy experience, Edmund would not react with such immediate urgency upon hearing he is to be sent away again. His haste to put his plan into immediate action justifies the belief it was a cold and loveless experience. This separation explains his need for his father's love. Inheriting his father's title and estate will prove his father's acceptance. Specifically examine the effects of this physical and emotional separation.

The lack of feminine care and nurturing plays an important role in his dealings with women. He offers unconditional loyalty to Nature and deceit and manipulation to Regan and Goneril. This dichotomy in feelings toward these three females expresses Edmund's ambivalence toward women. His feelings of abandonment by his mother have left scars. These feelings and his father's treatment of him have created a distaste for humanity, which is displayed in his ability to put his plan into action and wreak havoc on all around him.

Serafina

Sicily is a strict Catholic country, which accounts for Serafina's deeply held religious beliefs. Sicilian women live for their men, as displayed by her holding onto Rosario even after death. It offers insight into her behavior to Rosa over Jack and Rosa's experiences at school. Her lack of formal education makes Rosa's graduation very important to her. Rosa's education fills Serafina with pride and makes it important for her to attend Rosa's graduation.

She straddles the fence between the old and new worlds. By holding onto her old world beliefs, she is a woman torn between the safety of the old world's customs and beliefs and the call of the new world, with its risks and opportunities. These opposing forces create another area of conflict in a situation she is unable to rectify.

To augment Rosario's salary, she refined her sewing skills after Rosa's birth. This work also helped with her language skills, communication with others, and acclimation to her new world.

The defiance, piety, love, warmth, innocence, strength, and beliefs in the new and old are a complex mix of historical events in her life, creating surprises in her behavior, often even to herself.

Beneatha

Beneatha was born soon after the stock market crash of 1929 and raised during the Great Depression. Before she was a teenager, the United States was in World War II. She has experienced much deprivation in her twenty years.

After World War II, there was a feeling of needing to achieve in the country. The American dream was heard all across the country. People believed a college degree would better their lives and the lives of their children. Veterans were going to college on the GI Bill. Beneatha embraced the belief that with hard work you can achieve what you want in America.

Beneatha's will, strength, and pride were ingrained in her by her parents, both hard-working, proud African Americans. Her brother, Walter Lee, is fifteen years older. The difference in their ages made her the baby in the household. She got attention any way she could. Her need for attention is the precursor of her present behavior and demands to be heard. Beneatha enjoys the shock effect created by her sense of self.

The Youngers have lived on the South Side of Chicago in a poor African-American ghetto most of their lives. Having to share a bathroom with the neighbors makes her angry at her environment. The various deprivations she has experienced have added to her drive and ambition. The family's work ethic has set an example, giving her the discipline to work hard. She also knows her life will be changed for the better once she is through with school.

As an African American college student, it is clear Beneatha has diligently applied herself to her studies. She works hard and is a good student. Her desire to become a doctor makes her a unique, one-of-a-kind person. She is a trailblazer and willing to move through the world against all opposition.

At an early age, she realized she wanted to be a doctor and understood what it would take to rise to the challenge. The support she receives from her mother and her father (from what is known of him) helped instill in her a need for self-expression and growth. Beneatha enjoys her adventuresome spirit.

Her feminist attitudes are derived from influences at school, from the political turmoil in the African-American community, and from the unrest women were beginning to display openly.

Beneatha's drive and ambition demands and earns respect from her family.

Peter

Peter was born soon after World War II into an upper middle class, Italian-American family. Americans were striving to better themselves and move up the social and economic ladder. Peter's family instilled the importance of education in him.

Peter's use of literary and musical references says he spent a great deal of his formative and teenage years reading and listening to music. He probably did not spend much time playing with other children, perhaps in reaction to his father's desire for him to be more interested in sports than in books.

There is a sense of formality and standoffishness in Peter that very likely came from his upbringing and his being educated at a private academy.

Aware of his homosexuality at an early age, he dismissed it as a passing phase. Certainly, being raised Catholic did not allow him to explore or accept it. He probably experimented at Williams and discovered it was not a passing fancy. His Catholicism caused an internal struggle over whether to live as a homosexual. This struggle appears to have remained with him, but he let go of his Catholic upbringing when he chose to live as a gay man.

Peter's jump from liberal arts to science may have been influenced by his knowledge he would not have children of his own. His is a caring and nurturing personality, well suited to pediatrics.

Living in the Present (Now)

You have developed a history, or past, and brought your character into the present, the now. The writer gives your character a present by creating her or his circumstances and situation. Add your character's emotional truth and reality to get the present.

Edmund

His circumstance is to live in the eighth century BC. He has just returned from nine years in exile at school. Edmund is the illegitimate younger son of the Earl of Gloucester. His status caus-es him to feel unloved and means he is banned from inheriting his father's title and a share of the estate.

His immediate situation is that moments earlier, he was intro-duced by his father, to the Earl of Kent, a stranger. In making the introduction, Gloucester expressed his embarrassment at Edmund's very presence, ever reminding him of his infidelity.

I have so often blushed to acknowledge him.

With these words Gloucester reawakens Edmund's emotional pain. It has been dormant while he was away at school. Like a bell bonging in his ears, Edmund hears,

BASTARD! BASE!!!

The feeling is alive as a headache with no relief. These are words he has lived with all of his life, rendering him less than his brother Edgar and a second-class citizen to all society. He is on fire with rage.

The very next moment, Gloucester expresses love for Edmund and also immediately announces Edmund will be sent away again.

Edmund realizes his presence represents Gloucester's very public infidelity and that he must take immediate action. He views his brother Edgar as his true rival.

The next time we meet Edmund, later that same day, he deliv-ers his talk to Nature, hoping to permanently alter his life.

Serafina

Her circumstance is that she and her daughter, Rosa, live in a Sicilian-populated village on Louisiana's Gulf Coast in 1950. It is a hot and humid environment. Three years have past since her hus-band, Rosario, was killed in a truck crash, leaving her in a severe depression. She has built a protective wall around herself and refuses to move forward in her life.

The immediate situation is that it is Rosa's high school gradua-tion day and Serafina is late. She is hurriedly dressing when Flora and Bessie arrive to collect a blouse Flora has paid Serafina to make for her. Their insistence and their threat of exposure for working without a licence pressure her into finishing the blouse.

Beneatha

Her circumstance is that her family, the Youngers, have been packing to move. Her friend, Asagai, arrives, finding the apartment in a state of disarray. The packing has halted because of the loss of the inheritance money that was to pay for the move as well as Beneatha's medical education.

The immediate situation is that the loss of the money leaves Beneatha emotionally empty and numb. With the money gone, there is no chance of her continuing her education. Her dreams for her future are over. She sits with Asagai, feeling emptiness because of what has been taken away from her.

Peter

His circumstance is that it is 1974 on Richard Nixon's resignation day. Peter arrives at the Chicago Art Institute where his friend Heidi is taking part in a feminist protest rally. She phoned Peter to say hello and tell him she had no time to see him. Peter shows up to see her.

The immediate situation is that Peter arrives hurt and angry. Heidi has time for her political activities but none to see her closest and dearest friend. Peter is horrified at what he views as Heidi's emotional detachment from herself. He needs to inform her she can't take their relationship for granted.

Moving Toward a Future (Dreams and Goals)

The future is a motivating force. It directs and focuses you. The future creates forward movement and offers hope. Hope enhances your survival instincts. Together, hope and dreams get you through bad times.

Explore all aspects of your future. Examine how it colors your present and what it brings into your everyday, moment-to-moment existence. The dreams for your future bring a larger picture to your life.

Dreams help your character find her specific and definite motivations. Your character takes actions toward achieving her goals and objectives.

Edmund

Edmund's dreams are acceptance, a title, and his share of his father's estate. These are his immediate dreams. Edmund also dreams of becoming king. By marrying either Regan or Goneril, both presently married, he will inherit their realms and become king. Total acceptance by the world will be his. These needs and dreams drive and motivate his actions. Justifiably, he is doing this to feel equal to his peers.

Serafina

Serafina's dreams of a future died with Rosario and her miscarriage. Her dreams for the future are placed on her daughter, Rosa. Serafina's conscious future appears to be holding onto Rosario's love and reexperiencing their passion. His ashes represent this part of her future.

Subconsciously, she would like to be reawakened to a new expression of love. She protects herself from this dream not coming true by building barriers and defenses.

Beneatha

Beneatha dreams of becoming a doctor and healing people. Her dreams for her future are real. She is going to better herself, live a richer, more productive life than the other members of her family.

She wants more than just to become a doctor. She wants to show the world an African-American woman can make the American dream of hard work leading to success work for her. She wants to lift her race and gender to equality. The money may have evaporated due to stupidity, but her dreams remain strong and real. She is able to deal with the negativity around her because she has dreams.

Peter

Peter's dream is to be a doctor who makes a contribution to mankind. He dreams of a world of equality, respect, and consideration for all people: men, women and gays. He dreams of a time when AIDS will no longer exist. Peter's dreams also include a healthy relationship shared with the man of his dreams.

Equality is an important issue to him. He has a large appetite and wants it all. His dreams include a career, a long-term relationship, and rewarding friendships. Peter works hard for his dreams and manages to fulfill many of them.

Explore your character's dreams. Belief in dreams is larger than a self-centered need. Examine the strength it takes to move toward these dreams and beliefs. Creating change and opening people's eyes to truth and honesty is very difficult. Most people live in fear and wish to keep the status quo. People with dreams create change and better the lives of man.

The future affects your character. Knowing the dreams and hopes your character lives with gives importance and urgency to the moment. Your character's future is a driving force in moving him toward fulfilling his objective and in traveling along his emotional journey. Your character's dreams and future carries him past the end of the play.

Adopting a Persona

Marilyn Monroe's innocent sexuality, Johnny Depp's ambiguous sexuality, Diane Keaton's kooky vulnerability, Hugh Grant's self-effacing charm, Susan Sarandon's intelligent sensuality, and Sean Penn's streetwise intensity all qualify as personas, effective images exposing and protecting at the same time. A persona is the person the world recognizes. Sometimes it is the truth, often not. A persona may easily conceal the personal truth.

A persona is how you appear in the world: "The good child," "the happy-go-lucky girl," or "the self-sufficient guy." These are partly real, partly fabricated images getting you through most situations in life, sometimes knowingly, sometimes not. Like a second skin, your persona is invisible to you.

Many people adopt an opposite persona from their true nature. A vulnerable person may choose a persona of strength and self-sufficiency. Likewise, independent, strong-willed people may want to appear vulnerable. People are known by their personas and accepted for these qualities. It is only with familiarity and insight that others begin to see cracks in these images, cracks that reveal the truth.

Characters live life with personas, an image protecting and exposing them as they wish to be experienced and known.

Edmund

Edmund adopts a persona of confidence and strength, a take-charge man. His persona makes him appear invulnerable to the world. Self-sufficient, independent, capable of reaching the heights is how he wants the world to view him. His persona hides his need to be loved and accepted.

Serafina

Serafina's persona is of a grieving Sicilian widow with defiance and strength. Beneath this persona is a passionate woman yearning to be emotionally fulfilled: desiring to love and be loved, vulnerable and needy. Serafina masks these truths from all around her. She plays the grieving widow card at every opportunity.

Beneatha

Beneatha's persona is to appear as a force of nature, like a warrior covered in armor. Humor is her armor. She hides behind her persona to deal with the truth of her circumstance. With the loss of her education money, she exposes the hurt and pain she hid via her persona. Her persona was helping her fulfill her dreams and move toward the future.

Peter

Peter's adopted as a persona a solid, caring, and successful man. He presents himself as literate, charming, and completely together. His persona protects him from man's inhumanity to man.

Personas are adopted to protect from pain and hurt. Personas help these characters remain alive in the world and reach their objectives.

Arriving at Decisions

Arriving at decisions is not easy. Decisions play a significant role in life. Think how many decisions people make each day. Decisions activate their internal lives, their reasoning. Explore the decision-making process. There is usually an inner struggle, should I or shouldn't I, before arriving at a decision. Everyone handles the process differently. Decisions are made in the moment; once the decision is accepted, people move quickly.

Awareness of the time needed to reach a decision is an important aspect of arriving at a decision. Taking the steps makes it clear for the audience. Slow down. Explore each factor involved. Taking the necessary steps and time to fulfill the moment brings clarity to understanding your decision. Decisions reveal the inner conflict your character has to work through.

Allow your character to resist making her decision until the very moment she arrives there. This gives her an obstacle to overcome and creates an inner struggle. Allow her to fight against it until she knows it is the right decision. Choosing not to make a decision is also a decision. Doing nothing is a possibility. Arriving at a decision is an inner activity that keeps your character alive at every moment.

Edmund

Edmund calls upon Nature to help him arrive at his decision: Should I give this letter to my father? Do I want to pursue this line of action? Will I be able to deal with the ramifications? He needs to live this questioning process moment-by-moment until he arrives at an answer.

Edmund's inner conflict causes him to work himself into a frenzy, concluding his argument with the strongest reasons of all.

> *Well, my legitimate, if this letter speed*
> *And my invention thrive, Edmund the base*
> *Shall top th' legitimate. I grow, I prosper*
> *Now, gods, stand up for bastards!*

Edmund arrives at his decision with his last line. Until this moment, he struggles to make his decision concerning his plan.

Serafina

Serafina is confronted by Flora and Bessie. She begins by sharing her pride in her relationship.

> *At night I sit here and I'm satisfied to remember, because I had the best.—Not the third best and not the second best, but the* first *best, the* only *best!*

Realizing this is not enough, she decides to offer her truthful feelings and reveal herself.

> *The number of nights I held him all night in my arms. Sometimes I didn't sleep, just held him all night in my arms.*

Her decision rekindles the deep feelings she had stored away. Feelings she had tried not to think about or feel for years, only to be awakened by her explanation to Flora and Bessie.

From their reactions, she can tell they have no interest in what she is sharing. In defiance, she takes time and arrives at a decision to toss their tawdriness in their faces.

> *Go on, you do it, you go on the streets and let them drop their sacks of dirty water on you!*

Her decision helps her hide from the deep feelings she has just rekindled.

Beneatha

Under Asagai's penetrating eyes and simple question, Beneatha arrives at her decision to share herself honestly.

> *Me, I'm nothing.*

With these words, Beneatha is newly born. She decides to share with him a story she has lived with herself. She has never shared the effects of this experience with anyone. Her decision proves to be life affirming.

Reawakening to her dreams about the medical profession, she takes a beat to think about these feelings. As the old power surges inside her again, Beneatha feels the need to protect herself from these old feelings.

> *. . . it doesn't seem deep enough, close enough to what ails mankind! It was a child's way of seeing things—or an idealist's.*

Beneatha will not allow herself to be hurt again. She defends herself against feeling her deep-seated need to heal and cure. She decides to save herself from even greater hurt.

Peter

Peter's realization of the depth of Heidi's detachment from him forces him to decide to tell her how he is feeling toward her.

> *Actually, I'm afraid I'm feeling sort of distant from you. I'm not criticizing you. It's just how I'm feeling.*

Heidi's indifference drives Peter to make a decision to reveal himself for the first time. Unaware of how she will take his news, he decides to go ahead and take the risk.

> *Heidi, I don't play on your team.*

Again no reaction, prompting him to proceed and try to shake her up.

> *I've become a liberal homosexual pediatrician.*

Whether she gets it or not, at this point Peter is open and honest with her. His decisions have forever altered their relationship.

Decisions can be life changing. They create openness and vulnerability, and bring danger to the moment, danger the other person will reject the information. This raises the stakes.

The decision-making process happens in the moment. It has steps that need to be fulfilled to clearly communicate the inner emotional movement. Decisions create new emotional experiences for your character and the other person. They are new because it is the first time either person has been there.

Awakening to Discoveries

Discoveries are a many splendored asset. They provide light in the darkness awakening your character to previously undisclosed answers. They clarify confusion, open new areas of exploration, and bring unrealized insights. Discoveries happen in the moment, keeping your character alive in her present.

Discoveries allow your character to gain insights. When the lightbulb of discovery goes on, your character and the audience bond in the moment. Creating this bond rallies it to root for your character to reach her objective. Discoveries spring from your character's psyche. Unexpectedly, they can explode when your character is searching for the next thing to say or the next place to take the other person on the emotional journey.

Discoveries can be moments of enlightenment: moments of remembering old thoughts and beliefs or realizations about yourself or the other person. They can have a variety of effects. There is always an effect, and it is usually immediate. One effect is grounding your character in the precise moment of the discovery.

Discoveries differ from remembering. Remembering is recalling the past. Remembering takes you back to your past. Discoveries are instantaneous new thoughts adding fresh fuel to your character's arguments. Discoveries happen only in the moment.

Explore moments when you could not come up with an answer, were not clear about what next step to take. Suddenly, a thought pops into your head, clarifying and focusing your thoughts. These are discoveries made in the moment. Examine how they make you feel and how they happen. Consider the time they take to become part of your being. How does your body feel when you are helped to move to another place by the illumination offered by the lightbulb going on?

It may be something you were trying to figure out yesterday. Discoveries often happen like a flash out of the blue. You probably were not even involved with this issue when the answer came to you. This is the beauty of a discovery.

Let the discovery affect you emotionally, physically, and spiritually. Be sure to fulfill the necessary steps discoveries take. Use the time needed. This awareness allows your character to be alerted to his discoveries and to communicate them clearly.

Edmund

Edmund calls upon Nature with ideas about what he will say to her, but does not have a prepared speech. His subconscious helps him.

> *... to thy law my services are bound.*

This instantaneous thought is a discovery. He tells Nature he will do whatever she says. This discovery delights him. His commitment will bring Nature to his aid in making the right decision. At the same time, it allows him to place the responsibility of the after-effects totally on Nature's shoulders, relieving him of any blame.

Serafina

Expressing the depth of her love, Serafina discovers how alive the experience still is in her.

> *Four thousand—three hundred—and eighty.*

As these words are spoken, Serafina discovers her entanglement with her past. This discovery of knowing the specific number excites her, excites her by knowing she has made the right decision in holding onto the past. There will never be a love like this for her again.

As she nears the end of her speech, she is struck with the discovery of being awakened to all the feelings she believed were in her past, feelings and sensations she thought she had successfully put to rest.

> *I'm satisfied to remember the love of a man that was mine—only mine! Never touched by the hand of nobody! Nobody but me!—Just me! Never nobody but me!*

Being awakened by her discoveries, she experiences the rawness of being without Rosario. These discoveries force her to tamp down her rising feelings. Serafina recoils into her state of denial and returns to what has become her life.

Beneatha

Beneatha has no answer to Asagai's question. She repeats his words a number of times, stalling until the lightbulb of her true feelings goes on and she decides to share her truth with him.

> *. . . I'm nothing.*

This discovery startles her. She has always had faith in the superiority of her intellect, humanity, and strength. Her confident persona is shattered. The discovery stops her in the moment. She is not sure how to proceed, where to go, or what to do.

Later she makes another discovery:

> *I wanted to do that. I always thought it was the one concrete thing in the world that a human being could do.*

She is taken aback by the depth of feelings it stirs in her. This last discovery is revelatory. It returns her to the vision she had that day, a vision of what she wanted to do in her life. This discovery reawakens her to her belief in medicine and its universal healing power, along with man's ability to help mankind.

Beneatha discovers her calling is to heal. She needs to find a way to achieve this objective with or without the help of her father's insurance money.

Peter

In his first moment, Peter sees a side of Heidi he had never seen before. It is like seeing her for the first time.

What a perky Seventies kind of gal you are!

This is a discovery of revelation. He does not recognize this empty and detached Heidi as the close friend he loves. He uses his sense of humor to get him through this discovery and be able to move on to the next moment.

His discovery prompts him to look at his own life and quickly decide on what is important to him. What he discovers is his feelings for this Heidi are not the same as his feelings for his other Heidi.

Actually I'm afraid I'm feeling sort of distant from you.

This discovery informs him of the truth, allowing him to breath and pull his thoughts together. A new discovery pops into his head. "Tell her the truth." He proceeds

I've become a liberal homosexual pediatrician.

He discovers it has had the effect of allowing him to accept his homosexuality openly. This discovery, from out of the blue, surprises him. It also relieves him of the unrealized weight he has been carrying on his shoulders.

Discoveries have different effects and serve many purposes. They surprise, awaken, rekindle, and maybe even open doors you never knew were closed. They can pop into your character's mind and enlighten him to the truth he has been searching for.

Understanding Character Adjustments

Characters make many adjustments to help them cope with difficult people, situations, and events. Each character responds in her or his own way. Some of these adjustments have been part of their emotional makeup while others happen in the moment.

Characters also have to make a variety of adjustments emotionally to protect themselves. Should they hide or reveal their emotional truths? What should they choose to reveal in any given moment?

Building Your Character's Cover

First, there is the character's cover. The cover is an internal emotional response to a difficult situation or person you consciously choose not to reveal yourself to.

Your finger is poised to ring the bell. "Why did I agree to show up here?" goes through your head. "Idiot!!" comes a reverberating voice from the cavernous inside of your head.

Your ex is inside with her new partner. You were prepared to handle this experience when the invite came, but now you would like to be anywhere else. You want to run. Instead, you take a deep breath and push the ringer. From inside the apartment, you hear the buzzer. Suddenly the door opens. You flash a big smile and say, "Hello." Your eyes dart among the guests to see if the path is clear to get a drink and relax.

You have covered your true feelings, made an adjustment to disguise your truth in the moment. The cover helps you cope with a difficult situation or person. It helps you begin to lose track of how you truly feel. The cover becomes real. You begin to feel as the cover prescribes.

Edmund

Edmund calls on Nature for help. Asking for help makes him feel emotionally uncomfortable. He presents a confident, warm, and friendly cover to her. If Edmund was truly self-confident, he would activate his plan without needing confirmation from anyone.

This cover hides his feelings of insecurity and self-loathing. He is the little boy screaming, "Love me, love me, please love me. Stop me from being illegitimate, a bastard." His cover quells his inner voice.

Laying it out for Nature and convincing himself at the same time, he wins on both counts. He and Nature believe the cover before them. It becomes his emotional truth in this moment.

Serafina

Serafina tries to mobilize herself to get dressed for Rosa's graduation. Her depression and lethargy slow her down. Flora and Bessie arrive, and Serafina adopts the cover of a caring mother needing to get to her daughter's graduation. Flora threatens her with exposure to the authorities for working without a license. Serafina acquiesces to her demand and works on Flora's blouse. The two taunt Serafina, who covers with her triumphant Sicilian widow persona.

Her speech brings her cover and her inner feelings together as one, and in the moment Serafina believes her own cover.

Beneatha

Following the loss of the family money, Beneatha feels numb and worthless. When Asagai asks her about herself, she lamely tries to cover her emotional emptiness with questions but fails. She lets the cover drop and reveals her feeling of nothingness.

Unable to deal with this exposed vulnerability, Beneatha covers her feelings by becoming a storyteller. In the course of the story, the cover overtakes her, and she becomes involved in the discovery of her own truth. By the end of her story, her cover has freed her from the feelings of nothingness and allows her to move forward in the moment.

Peter

Peter's immediate emotional response to Heidi's declaration of emotional and sexual compartmentalization is infuriation. He immediately adopts a cover of humor to distract her from his true feelings toward her.

It lasts only a few moments. His fury and her indifference are so strong he cannot hold onto this cover. He keeps recovering his humor, making a conscious adjustment to cover his fury so he can reach Heidi.

Each character uses cover in his own way to allow him to proceed, remain in control, and focus on the objective. The words your character speaks are, more often than not, his cover.

Living In Denial

Denial is a defense used to block out a truth characters find too painful to live with. Denial is used to hide from themselves. It defends against the loud internal voice coming from their subconscious. Denial allows them to feel better about themselves, their situation, and often, their total existence.

Explore your character's state of denial. Ask yourself the following questions to understand the truth behind the denial. What is she in denial about? Did she do something she wants to forget? What is she hiding from herself? The answer will be different for each character.

Edmund

Edmund denies there is an alternative to his plan for achieving his objective. He denies the truth of the effects his action will have on his family and society. Denial helps him cope with the formality, savagery, and brutality of the time and allows him to move forward.

Blinded by the pain of the circumstances surrounding his birth, his denial allows him to justify his course of action and convince himself it is the true way to proceed.

Serafina

Serafina refuses to hear anything from anyone about Rosario's possible infidelity. Her denial grows stronger as Flora and Bessie taunt her. Her denial causes her to move in defiance and behave triumphantly.

Her denial allows her to hold onto her beliefs about their shared monogamous love. Serafina's denial is reinforced with each penetrating comment about the truth.

Beneatha

Beneatha's denial of the truth comes at the end of her speech when she is confronted with the potency of her feelings about becoming a doctor. Denial is her only salvation. It allows her to minimize the pain of truth.

She spits out the word "idealist" as if it is a dirty word. She uses it to help regain her strength.

Peter

Peter's fury at Heidi's indifference, along with his realization of her emotional detachment, is so strong he is unable to find the energy to deny any of it. His intelligence and self-awareness do not allow him to use denial as a defense.

Characters use denial in one way or another at different times. Eventually, they are forced to open themselves to their denial and face the truth of their emotional needs.

Having Secrets

A secret is something only your character knows. It can be something he is aware of or something he has chosen to hide from himself. Either of these decisions colors your character's behavior. The addition of a secret to his emotional makeup adds another dimension of complexity.

Secrets, by their very nature, are not shared with others. They can be secrets your character does not want to share, is ashamed to share, or is waiting for the right moment to surprise the other person. Secrets can be positive or negative. They can be good or bad. Secrets create mystery in your character. Secrets are private to your character and need never be revealed.

Secrets affect many aspects of your character and bring variety and different shadings to moments. A secret can add subtlety to a choice. By choosing the right secret for your character, her choices, decisions, and actions become more specific. Having a secret may even justify your character's actions.

Edmund

Edmund's secret is his love for Cordelia. She is the one daughter of King Lear he has always enjoyed being with. He played with her when they were children before he was sent away to school. He enjoyed her sense of fairness. Cordelia believes in Nature and introduced Edmund to its power.

King Lear will never allow her to marry the illegitimate Edmund. She is a daughter of the king of the realm. Edgar, yes. Edmund, no. If Edmund disgraces Edgar in the eyes of one and all and gains his father's title and estate, he has a chance to be given Cordelia's hand. In the end, his true feelings toward Cordelia win out as he hurriedly tries to save her.

This secret adds another personal and positive motivation to Edmund's plan.

Serafina

Serafina's secret is her subconscious belief in Rosario's infidelity. She senses it by the hours he kept when he was alive. She feels it when she walks into the living room and finds Estelle Hohengarten holding his picture and offering her the rose-colored silk.

Her secret adds to the strength and power of her denial and her need for her cover of defiant triumph.

Beneatha

Beneatha's secret is to win the Nobel Prize in Medicine. She wants to be the first African-American woman to be heralded as a great scientist and person. She will cure mankind's ills, especially man's inhumanity to man.

This secret keeps her on her path, heightening the importance of Walter Lee's loss of the inheritance. Secretly believing she will be the most important doctor in the world and having it taken away from her compounds the nothingness she experiences.

Peter

Peter's secret is his desire to share his life with Heidi and have children with her. Peter convinces himself there is truth to this secret. It increases his anger and frustration whenever he sees, or

Heidi talks about, Scoop. It also adds more pain to his feelings about his homosexuality.

This secret makes everything about Heidi and their relationship more important. It is a motivating factor in his fury at her indifference.

Secrets add a layer of importance to your character. They guide you to more definite and specific choices. They justify decisions and actions and add a layer of mystery to your character. Secrets color your character's subtext, inner life, choices, decisions, actions, and future.

Coping with Physical Activities

There are also character adjustments of a physical nature. These physical activities, often prescribed by the author, alter the way characters behave in the situation and/or circumstance in the moment.

Edmund

Edmund has just heard he will be sent away again. This creates an urgency, both physical and emotional. He needs to get a speedy response from Nature but not make her feel pressured.

This adjustment brings an interesting color to his speech. On the one hand, he needs an immediate response before it is too late. On the other, he wants her to feel she can take the time she needs to weigh and balance both sides of his issue. It offers him the chance to play both sides. Do it now, but don't rush.

Serafina

Serafina's lethargy causes her to move and perform chores slowly. Depression and lack of concern have taken over these last three years. Hearing the high school band warming up creates an urgency in Serafina, forcing herself to respond against her lethargy. She increases her speed and energy in her need to find the Bulova watch she bought for Rosa as a graduation present.

Flora's demands that Serafina finish her blouse create adjustments she has to make in her physical activities.

She has to look for the watch. She has to pull herself together and get dressed. And now, she has to sew the pieces of the blouse together. Each of these activities are done one at a time. She searches. She thinks, Where did I put that watch? What am I going to wear? How can I spend time finishing this blouse? She sews. Carefully but with rapidity. She moves from one to the other and back again. All the while the minutes are moving the graduation closer. These activities add to the emotional layers already at play.

Beneatha

Beneatha's natural rhythm is fast. Here she is talking to Asagai and feeling wounded, vulnerable, and lost. She is not able to hide behind her normally high-energy persona. She makes a physical adjustment to slow down, to hold onto herself, to say and do the right thing. She forces herself to take one step at a time and not get her ahead of herself for fear of losing it. This brings a precision to Beneatha not previously seen.

This physical adjustment informs of the depth of hurt she is experiencing.

Peter

Peter stands in the rain in a vast open area. He makes a physical adjustment to the rain by opening his umbrella. The act of holding the umbrella and dealing with the emotional content of the moment creates a physical handicap.

Wishing to have this intimate conversation in a private place, Peter has to physically adjust to the wide open space he is forced into. He can't whisper. She will never hear him. Her indifference and unwillingness to pay attention to what he is telling her causes him to speak louder. Add to this the milling of people around them. Peter is out of his element and adjusts accordingly.

Physical activities are adjustments each character makes to fulfill the truth of the moment. Characters do not change their choices but add the necessary physical adjustments, focusing themselves and moving toward their desired objective.

Don't change your choices to accommodate someone or something added to the situation or circumstance. Rather, you broaden the mix. Adding creates layers. Layering creates complexity and interest.

Overcoming Obstacles

Overcoming obstacles adds to the inner and outer struggle your character goes through. They are the actor's best friend by creating a stronger need to fight to reach her objective. Obstacles limit her odds against reaching her goal. It raises the stakes, keeping her inner struggle alive in the moment.

Don't minimize your character's obstacles. Make them seem large. A difficult obstacle offers your character an active and urgent need to combat it. Your character's need creates variety in her methods of fighting to rid herself of these obstacles and achieve her objective.

Edmund

Edmund's obstacle is Edgar's legitimacy. It prevents Edmund from receiving their father's love and approval. It stands in the path of Edmund's inheriting his share of their father's realm and the title. Edmund loves Edgar, but his love is overshadowed by the ever-present legitimacy/illegitimacy issue that separates them. The love Edmund feels toward Edgar creates an emotional vise tightening around him.

Edmund's obstacle is large and hangs over him at all times. Edgar is the ever-present, bigger-than-life elephant in the room.

Fine word, "legitimate"!

He needs to rid himself of the sight and sound of this word to restore peace to his soul. He speaks of the "plague of customs."

His choice of the word "plague" describes the enormity of his illegitimacy in his life. It is not a problem, not an illness, but a plague. His emotional pain caused by this plague is palpable. Edmund carries his illegitimacy around like a deformity for all to see.

The curiosity of nations.

He feels he is in a fish bowl with everyone peering at him: *Illegitimate!!!* He feels he is a freak in a freak show, stared at by one and all. All of this is perpetrated by Edgar's existence. Edmund's need to overcome his obstacle is alive in every minute.

Serafina

Rosario is the obstacle Serafina fights not to overcome. Her love for Rosario did not end with his death. His ever-present ashes keep him alive. She is determined to keep him with her even in death.

> *At night I sit here and I'm satisfied to remember, because I had the best.—Not the third best and not the second best, but the* first *best, the* only *best!—So now I stay here and am satisfied now to remember, ...*

Serafina is obstinately determined to bring her obstacle into her future. Keeping Rosario alive prevents her from having to learn if there is any truth to the suspicions about him and Estelle.

When he was alive, she dressed for him and kept herself looking beautiful. Now she has no need to. He is always with her. Keeping Rosario with her prevents her from having to think about her future. She has her future, Rosario until death.

Letting go of Rosario, facing the truth about his infidelity, and moving into her future could be achieved if she overcame her obstacle. Serafina has no desire to overcome her obstacle. She has no need for the outside world to touch her. She fights everyone to hold onto her obstacle, preventing herself from moving on.

Beneatha

Beneatha's obstacle is her family. She loves her family, and as difficult as it is, she respects them. Their lack of support and belief in her dreams drive her to defend herself against the others attempts to minimize her. Their desire for assimilation, to keep the status quo, and for her to marry George make them her obstacle.

Her obstacle is ever present, respected, and loved. It's an obstacle difficult to overcome.

Peter

Peter's obstacle is Heidi's indifference. He cares deeply for her. What Peter finds when he arrives is a person totally obsessed with her career and political issues, a person compartmentalized and living a life devoid of emotional involvement or content, a person who believes in the importance of sexual relationships but with little interest in platonic ones, and a person involved in her work and the feminist movement at the expense of her emotional development. Peter tries to overcome this obstacle with humor, truth, and revelations about himself—all to no avail.

Arriving at his breaking point, Peter finds himself in a desperate need to reach her before their relationship dissolves. He resorts to a mix of hysteria, humor, honesty, and politics.

> *And* my *liberation,* my *pursuit of happiness, and the pursuit of happiness of other men like me is just as politically and socially valid as hanging a couple of Goddamned paintings because they were signed by someone named Nancy, Gladys, or Gilda. And that is why I came to see you today. I am demanding your equal time and consideration.*

Heidi finally hears him. She begins to understand his serious need for her attention. He has reached her. It appears he has overcome his obstacle.

Obstacles are important. They offer your character an active inner fight and conflict, keeping him alive in the moment. Obstacles are created either by your character, his circumstance, his situation, or another character. Overcoming obstacles frees your character to focus on the bigger picture and continue on his emotional journey to reach his objective.

Activating Your Character's Inner Conflict: *The Fight Within*

Your inner conflict, or struggle, activates you. The push/pull sensation you experience makes you jumpy and edgy filling you with unrest and discord. These emotional conflicts keep you alive—maybe not happy, content, or comfortable—but active.

Explore your inner conflict. What is it about? Do you go back and forth after making a decision? Become aware of internal aspects activating and motivating you. You may not feel any outward manifestation of your inner conflict but experience the alive sensation it creates.

This inner conflict is an important part of your character's emotional makeup. The inner conflict breaks down the solidity of her emotionally protected self. It makes her appear vulnerable. Lack of certainty, important events, and big decisions are areas causing the fight within.

Edmund

Edmund's inner conflict is deeply embedded in his soul. His feelings of love for Edgar and his desire to soil Edgar's character create his profound inner conflict. This conflict is one of the motivating factors pushing him to seek Nature's guidance.

Edmund lives with much inner turmoil. Sibling rivalries for parental attention and love go back to Cain and Abel. In addition, his conflict with his father keeps him walking an emotional tightrope. His inner struggle, "should I or shouldn't I take this action?," moves him forward step by step. With each step he struggles, conflicted about which route to take. The conflict shows he is human: good and bad, loving and hating, needy and demanding.

Everyone has experienced the "Mom/Dad loves you more than they love me" argument. It is a universal conflict and something everyone can identify with once you make it personal and specific. It is not about land, greed, or anger, but a deeply rooted human need for love and acceptance.

Serafina

Serafina's inner conflicts are very strong and inform her every moment and decision. Was Rosario unfaithful or not? Did she do the right thing having him cremated? Has she behaved impiously to Our Lady? Will she have to pay the ultimate price of being alone forever?

All of these unanswered questions keep her on an unbalanced seesaw. She experiences up and down sensations most of the time: "I did the right thing. He was faithful. I did the wrong thing. He did have an affair with Estelle Hohengarten." As these thoughts circulate inside her, conflict grows stronger and needs to be continually suppressed.

This suppression causes her inner struggle to activate, keeping her emotionally alive at every moment. This inner conflict keeps the depression alive, adding to her need to live in denial. The denial helps numb the pain caused by her inner conflict.

These inner struggles keep Serafina fighting to calm them down and move to a feeling of peace and serenity.

Beneatha

Beneatha's inner fight is caused by her conflicted feelings about her family. Her dabbling in many areas of self-expression indicates conflicts about her decision to become a doctor. She questions herself about its truth and validity. Is this her true dream? Is this what she really wants?

Needing to appear strong in her beliefs to combat her family's taunts creates inner turmoil. Holding onto her dreams against their wishes for her to marry George and give them up activates her inner life. Beneatha has no one with whom to share these self-doubts and conflicts until her moment of total surrender with Asagai.

Beneatha's inner conflict saves her from slipping into self-pity when she tells her story to Asagai. She fights to uncover the truth of her dream and fights to keep it alive. She struggles to believe once and for all in her dream of becoming a doctor.

Peter

Peter's homosexuality paired with his love for Heidi creates an inner conflict. His need for Heidi causes him to fluctuate back and forth between accepting and rejecting his homosexuality. His homosexuality creates conflict with Scoop.

His homosexuality is not accepted by the church. Raised Catholic, he struggles with the church's rejection and his need to accept himself. This conflict creates positive and negative feelings—happy and sad, good and bad—involving him in an inner conflict for acceptance. There is no way for him to resolve this inner turmoil.

Relive the times you experienced the push/pull of your emotions. This inner activity creates discomfort. Make these struggles, fights, or conflicts personal and real within your character. Don't allow your character to feel comfortable. It creates inertia and allows her to appear complacent and boring. Dramatists never have a character in a comfortable place. There would be no drama. Discomfort creates angst and need. An inner conflict adds dis-ease, creating an active need to arrive at a place of peace. The inner conflict creates an active inner life.

Unearthing Your Character's Subconscious

Your character communicates his conscious feelings, ideas, and beliefs with words. His subconscious is what is communicated without words. Your character's subconscious plays a major role in layering his outer life with the subconscious effects in his inner life. It colors his conscious choices. His subconscious is comprised of both positive and negative words, thoughts, and moments from his past, present, and future. It contains secrets often never shared with or spoken to another person and often not even shared with or accepted by himself. It is imbedded in his psychological history. Some of it true, and some of it is believed and accepted without being fact based. His subconscious may be formed by lies and deceits or desires and wishes he has been told or created for himself.

Explore important facets of the subconscious feelings that drive you. Perhaps someone important tried to discourage you from following your dreams, instilling insecurities and doubt. Reawaken the truth of your emotional reaction. The effects are mixed and complex, consisting of bad and good feelings about yourself and your dreams. You are still an actor; you didn't succumb to others' opinions. But the words are imbedded in your subconscious. At times, it causes you to squelch your dreams; at others, it causes you to rise up and fight against the naysayers.

Subconscious feelings and thoughts exist. They are different for all people and characters, and all affect the psyche. Unearthing your character's subconscious brings specificity, justification, and truth to her conscious action and thoughts. Her subconscious is created through clues and information based on her emotional makeup, psychological needs, and behavior.

Edmund

Edmund's subconscious drives and confuses him. Is he a bastard? Are his character and personality defined by his illegitimacy? Yes and no. He lives with his father's voice, both clear and muted. Edgar never refers to him as illegitimate, but Edmund feels Edgar has thought it many times. Edmund's subconscious separates them. He subconsciously feels everyone thinks about his illegitimacy whenever they see him. Much of his energy is used to block out the powerful voices in his subconscious. He sees the words "Illegitimate" and "Bastard" branded on him in everyone's eyes and thoughts. Edmund's subconscious lives with this palpable pain and causes him to rise up and put his plan into action.

Serafina

Serafina appears to be a formidable woman. Subconsciously, she needs Rosario for strength to combat her inner demons. Subconsciously, she still carries her feelings of being a foreign child in a foreign land. The fierceness she displayed when having him cremated appears strong, but her subconscious need to keep him with her was really that of a needy child crying within.

Subconsciously, she knows Rosario was unfaithful to her and much energy goes to strengthening her denial. Her denial fights information that might penetrate her being. Her subconscious prevents this from happening. She chooses denial to keep her subconscious at bay. Her denial began as a conscious choice but has become a way of life.

Serafina has an active subconscious. It tries to permeate her conscious thoughts. Suppressing this truth keeps her activated and alive.

Beneatha

Beneatha actively keeps her subconscious thoughts removed from her consciousness. She behaves like a child of privilege, indulging in any form of self-expression she chooses. Her subconscious screams at her about the truth of her socio-economic situation. It forms her behavior by forcing her to be brash, irreverent, and defended.

With her bubble burst by Walter Lee's loss of the family money, she is forced to confront her subconscious. Relating her story to Asagai allows her to rebuild her belief one brick at a time. She regains her sense of empowerment from the truth of her convictions discovered in Rufus's story.

Peter

Peter's subconscious is filled with pain and self-loathing. He fights against it all the time. He outwardly accepts his homosexuality but subconsciously believes it is a sin. He wrestles with this issue all through the play.

His cynicism and humor are a direct result of his need to reject the feelings locked in his subconscious. They protect him from the pain inflicted on homosexuals by society. Pediatrics, caring for Heidi, and working for AIDS reform all express an idealistic nature bucking his loud subconscious voices.

Your character's subconscious affects how he feels about himself and others. His subconscious adds an element of discord to his personality. Subconscious feelings often bring an opposite response to what is expected from them. These unexpected moments add to your character's complexity. Putting the pieces together brings discoveries from his subconscious, often clarifying his behavior in the moment.

The subconscious is a major driving force affecting your character's personality. It adds layers of mystery, surprise, truth, and pain, creating internal action and unrest. The subconscious aids in keeping him alive and struggling.

Dialoguing Your Character's Subtext: Inner Monologue

The voice inside your head speaks your inner monologue. The familiar voice that admonishes, lauds, goads, corrects, and diminishes you is your subtext, or inner monologue. It is often called your conscience. Dialogue heard and retained from your past by parents, teachers, relatives, friends, and lovers helps create your subtext. Debating or questioning who you are, what you should do, how you should do it, and how qualified you are to do anything, your inner voice offers opinions on all facets of your life. It is sometimes your champion, sometimes your nemesis, but it is always with you creating an inner dialogue by sharing thoughts.

Become aware of your own inner monologue. It is always going on in your head, even when you are communicating with another person. These voices don't go away. They may subside for an instant, but you can never get too far away from them. It is very difficult to stop your subtext from offering opinions.

The inner monologue is universal. Meditation practices are used to quiet these voices. Buddhism teaches quieting the voices to reach your truth. This discipline speaks of the difficulty in quieting an inner voice. That inner monologue continually judges actions and deeds with both positive and negative feedback and distracts you from reaching your goals.

Use your inner monologue to fill out your thoughts. This helps commit you to your character when inhabiting her life. The monologue fills so much of your character's conscious and unconscious thoughts that it aids in ridding you of self-consciousness.

Your character needs an inner monologue and voice to create her inner struggle. Secrets can aid in creating inner voices.

Depending on your chosen secret, the power of the inner monologue can have a strong impact. The more you know about your character, the more information you can use to create a potent inner monologue.

The inner monologue is not linear but abstract, jumping from one topic to another. Thoughts and feelings come and go, floating through your character's inner self. Some land, some just float in space. The inner monologue and subtext are like a collage created from life, offering different segments at different moments. It takes a major effort to control the inner monologue.

It is important to know how your character arrived at her beliefs about God, religion, politics, education, and her feelings of self. Explore your character's truth from all aspects of her life for the widest range of subtextual material.

Edmund

Edmund is plagued with an inner monologue about his illegitimacy and his need to rectify this situation. The impact of his father's thoughts speak loud and clear in his subtext. This voice dominates his feelings about himself, creating a constant dialogue within about his own unworthiness. Add information given by other people, events, issues, and decisions to Edmund's inner monologue.

His feelings about being sent away and the people he lived with are inner thoughts. His abandonment by his mother adds to his inner voices about his feelings toward women. He has a running inner monologue about all aspects of his relationship with Edgar.

Edmund's inner monologue drives him to believe that activating his plan will get him the love and acceptance he craves. It tells him the plan will create an equality and shared acceptance with Edgar, giving him his deserved title and share of the estate.

Serafina

Serafina's subtext is composed of an inner struggle over Rosario's faithfulness, her belief in her religion, and her guilt about his cremation. Added to this are her thoughts about Our Lady's omnipresent feelings toward her, her unsureness in dealing with Rosa, and her fight to keep the truth in denial. These issues combine to create a powerful inner voice and monologue.

They come at her abstractly. Changing course at different moments and never remaining the same, they cause confusion and inner turmoil.

Her inner voices tell her she was bad and that was the reason Rosario was taken from her. They keep her in mourning by constantly reminding her of her guilt and her need for repentance because she had him cremated.

Beneatha

Beneatha's inner monologue is constantly fluctuating. It alternates between words of her superiority and attacks against her for her behavior toward her family. She has opposing feelings about Walter Lee. She loves him but wishes he would grow up. When she interacts with him, her inner monologue sometimes tells her to condemn him and other times to offer him solace. She loves her mother but wishes she would let go of this God stuff and understand the importance of science. Her beliefs in Darwin against creationism battles within. Her sister-in-law Ruth is an unexplored person. Beneatha does not comprehend the relationship shared by a married couple and is not happy about Ruth's acceptance of Walter Lee.

Her voices are disrespectful of George and his values. He is just a rich kid with no social redeeming values or concerns. On the other hand, he has security to offer and a bathroom of her own.

The ambivalence and ambiguity create loud voices she needs to drown out by keeping busy and combating them with humor. Her sense of herself is unsure, but she acts as if she is all the things she is trying to believe. Her inner monologue tells her differently.

Peter

Peter's inner monologue consists of his demons, feelings of humanitarianism, love, and intense disgust about his homosexuality while at the same time, he is fighting to accept it unconditionally. Peter's subtext is complex. His Catholic upbringing is in constant combat with his homosexuality. No matter how much he has cast off his religious beliefs, they are imprinted on him and alive in his subtexual conversations.

His feelings about Scoop are conflicted. He sees Scoop for who he is but wants to see the good side of him for Heidi's sake. His relationship with Stanley fulfills many needs but not all. These issues allow his conscience to support and condemn him.

His humor is both amusing and biting. He appreciates it at times and at others it disgusts him. His inner voices enjoy the effect they have on him. Peter's pain creates an inner monologue pushing him to let others know where he stands at all times and at all cost. Peter is not comfortable with this side of himself.

Your character's inner monologue and subconscious have strong reverberations in his present. Mixed dialogue, good and bad, color his conscious actions and choices. Take all his issues and the effects of each to bring the widest range in creating their dialogue for his specific inner monologue.

8

Believing in the Other Person

The other person, the person your character is talking to, holds the key to your character's achieving her objective. This makes the other person of paramount importance. Your character's need to reach her objective is her strongest drive. The other person's life-and-death importance to your character is created by the other's ability to help or hinder fulfilling the objective. Having this power over your character's outcome creates a moment-to-moment urgency.

Focus on the other person. Stay tuned to his every reaction. Coerce him into listening. Compel him to hear your character's reasoning. Scrutinize his every response carefully to be sure your character is convincing him of the truth of her arguments.

You, the actor, need to find the right emotional dynamic between your character and the other person. Explore the relationship between the two. Specify their feelings toward each other. This knowledge will pinpoint the route on which your character needs to take the other person to reach her objective.

Explore situations in your life of similar emotional dynamics to choose the correct person. One who arouses the same specific emotions will lead you to choose the right person. This person has the ability to fulfill your character's need.

Observe yourself in a situation in which you need something from another person. Examine how your emotional need makes you feel and behave. Recall how close attention invested in reading their responses helps you plan your next move. When you feel the other is not getting your points, discover how you change tactics to win the other over to your side.

Scrutinize the specific behavior of the other person. Awaken to how carefully you observe him. You see his hair, his eyes, and the clothes he is wearing with different eyes. The way he is sitting or standing becomes important in the moment. Notice the effect of a simple blinking of an eye when you are committed to getting help. Experience your intense responses to his every nuance. Feel the heightened apprehension when you do not get your needed response. Become aware of the weight being lifted when you feel he is in your corner. Bring these acute skills of observation to your monologue. When you are performing your monologue, the other person needs to be as specific in your mind's eye as when he is standing in front of you.

The more you, the actor, allow yourself to focus on the other person, the less aware you are of yourself. This allows you to fully commit to your actions and stay in the moment. You cannot achieve your objective alone. This intense awareness of the other character's responses compels you to live in the moment.

This is where your character's inner monologue comes into important play. It works concurrently with your awareness of the other person. Your character's inner voice informs you of the other person's reactions. Focusing on the other person's reactions to your arguments allows your character to make discoveries in the moment about how to proceed. This careful scrutiny and moment-by-moment response makes your character live each moment for the first time.

Keeping everything simple brings clarity to your communication with the other person. Your character is filled with complex needs. Define your character's specific need to communicate directly and simply with her.

When you are alone and you talk to yourself, you are doing a monologue. Examine the intensity of your focus. This importance on the other person communicates your need. This person is real in the moment. You may be talking to yourself, yet you believe and treat your other self as real as another person.

The joyful part of performing a monologue is creating another person who feeds you the needed reactions to proceed moment-by-moment along your character's emotional journey. Don't make it easy by allowing the other person to succumb to your character's need. Easing the difficulty gives your character less to fight against and muddles the dramatic effect. Create strong obstacles and resistance from the other person. The obstacles and resistance propels your character forward on his journey. The more you allow her to resist, the stronger your fight to win her over. The stronger your fight, the more importance and urgency you bring to each moment.

The emotional truth in the relationship between your character and the other person is the deciding factor in your choice of the other person. Investigate your history to experience your emotional truth when you are feeling vulnerable. Know the specific emotional needs of your character in choosing the correct dynamic in the relationship. Don't duplicate the physical relationship. Create the other person from the truth and honesty of the emotional relationship between these two people.

Edmund

Edmund's distrust of men and the lack of support he has experienced from them justifies his decision to choose Nature. She is an impartial woman whom he believes will bring this quality into play when he asks her help in making the right decision.

Edmund's selection of shared facts shows his reverence and belief in her omnipotent authority. He believes she will support him. The two possible outcomes are to proceed with his plan or not. His need is so great he convinces himself Nature has affirmed his plan.

It is important to understand Nature's importance to Edmund. If you are a person who prays, it will be simple to comprehend. If not, explore who or what you believe to be a higher power or being. The image you hold in your mind when you ask for help or clarity will create the correct emotional dynamic to use for communing with Nature.

Know this image specifically. Create it fully for yourself. Bring it to life to give Edmund someone to talk to and react with.

The relationship does not have to be identical. The emotional dynamic and its effect on you need to resonate. This emotional resonance is the necessary link in choosing the correct other person.

Serafina

Serafina talks to Flora and Bessie. Their relationship appears to be customer and seamstress yet she reveals intimacies about her life with Rosario. Look for the emotional dynamic causing Serafina to open to these women. They are the outside world, alive and fun loving. These are qualities Serafina has removed from her life since Rosario's death. These women hold the key to her subconscious dream and objective of being reawakened to her future.

Think about friends who tried to get you to go out in the world and meet someone new after an important breakup in your life. Remember how adamantly you refused. Recall their response and your emotional reaction to their persistence. The fear of letting go prevented you from opening up to new experiences and pleasure. You only remember the pain. This friend or acquaintance tells you of a party that may offer the fun you need back in your life. This opportunity creates a strong emotional push/pull. The more fun and joy the person expressed about life's possibilities, the harder you fought. This is what you need to bring to the other person to fulfill the needed truth in Serafina's monologue.

Moment by moment she is aware of how they are taking her words. Use their reactions to guide you on your emotional journey. If Serafina lets go of the belief she holds so dear, her world will crumble. She must convince them of her feelings. All the time she is protesting against the ideas, subconsciously she wants them to break down the hold Rosario's memory has on her.

Bring them to the monologue with you. See their reactions. Examine their physical presence. Know everything about them: their eyes, hair, smile. Each of these facets of their being will affect you and make the other persons real.

Beneatha

Asagai is very important to Beneatha. He believes in her dreams. He respects her. She respects him. He is awakening her to her African roots. There are romantic sparks between them, a feeling different from her feelings toward George. They connect intellectually, physically, spiritually, and culturally.

Asagai's influence on Beneatha is profound. He makes her reach into herself and see her soul. He touches something very deep in her, something beyond the material realm. He tests her, challenges her. He believes she can meet these tests and challenges. He reinforces her dream.

Asagai offers Beneatha the beauty and history of being African. He shares with her a more profound meaning of life, a life of giving, sharing, helping, and fulfilling her soul's desires.

Find in your history a person who instilled faith in you, a person who made you grow and reach for more than you ever believed you were capable of. People who instill faith, hope, and belief in you are people you love deeply, be it romantic, familial, or platonic. You cannot be affected strongly if love is not involved. Asagai affects Beneatha in ways beyond romance. He causes her to look into her soul, and to see what the value of life is about. He is a profound influence on Beneatha. This is the correct emotional makeup and motivation needed to choose the other person for Beneatha.

Beneatha shows Asagai a new and vulnerable side she has not shared with anyone. Beneatha's feelings in this moment are new to her. She is acutely aware of how Asagai is receiving this deeply felt sense of loss and defeat she is experiencing.

It is the effect the other person has on you that helps you fight through to his understanding. The more important you make him the easier it is to act with him. Choose someone who will test you. Fight you. Make you reach your depths of humanity. This is where Beneatha goes. Where she needs to be driven by the other person in order to open up.

Peter

Peter's other person is his closest friend, Heidi. She may mean more to him than Stanley Zinc, his boyfriend. His relationship with Heidi is complex and filled with many conflicted emotions. Peter's sense that Heidi fails to accept the importance of their friendship frustrates him. He needs to reach her, to arouse her to what she is doing to their relationship. His need is important enough for him to reveal truthful intimacies of his life on the steps of the Chicago Art Institute.

Choose a close friend, a friend whom you feel is misguided about a belief you feel strongly about. Awaken the emotions you experience whenever this subject arises. Relive the emotional drive you experience trying to get the person to understand your truth. This is the emotional dynamic needed to fulfill Peter's other person. It needs to be important for you to go as far as he does in trying to awaken Heidi.

Create the emotionally specific relationships for your characters by bringing real people into their monologue. See these people clearly. Remember their most distinct features. The more specific they are to you, the easier it will be to conjure up their reactions, which aid you in moving from one beat to the next, action by action. Take the other person on the emotional journey as your character actively tries to reach them. Change their way of thinking. Open them up to your character's needs. Convince them to look at what they are doing to their own life. Fight until the end. Make the other person understand. Be certain they are getting the message. If they are, adjust your character's next beat and action to their accepting point of view. If not, adjust your needs to the other person's negative point of view. Including all of these points, or as many as apply, will increase your ability to believe in the other person.

9

Shaping Your Monologue into a Three-Act Play

Creating an Emotional Arc

A good deal of subjective and introspective work has been done. You have created the inner and outer life of your character and sensorily awakened him to his environment. You have motivated and scrutinized his every action. You have psychologically and emotionally invested in his life. You have come to understand and interpret, through exploration of his needs and desires, the importance of his monologue.

Before you begin to perform your work, take an objective look at the truth, honesty, and complexity created by your work. Explore another aspect of the checks and balances involved, making sure no stone has been left unturned. Check that there are no holes in the carefully woven and multilayered character you have created. Be sure all aspects of his monologue have been attended to.

Your character's monologue is a microcosm of his world. It is a three-act play, a three-act play enveloping your character in a world specific and complete unto itself. Your character's life and environment are established and activated by pursuing his objective from a specifically defined emotional place (Act I). There is an emotional journey of actions, discoveries, events, arguments, and awarenesses (Act II). He arrives at a new emotional place having traveled the trajectory of his arc (Act III).

His emotional journey results in one of three possibilities. Reaching his objective brings him to a sense of fulfillment. Not achieving his objective brings him to a more desperate emotional space. Examining the results of achieving his objective, he may decide to remain where he began. This decision creates an emotional change to an acceptance of his situation or a state of denial. This acceptance leaves him without the angst-ridden drive. He is in a different emotional place. Any of these choices creates movement.

Taking NO action is an active choice. Your character chooses consciously or unconsciously to remain emotionally where she is. This is as important a choice as moving to a new place in her life. Moving from unacceptance to acceptance of the situation creates movement, change, and an emotional arc.

Taking steps to turn your speech into a three-act play focuses you clearly on the important needs of your character. It becomes clear why you are taking this journey. It also brings clarity to the reason you are talking to this specific other person and choosing to reveal what you do. It also helps specify what you need to do in each of the three acts.

Act I (The Beginning: Exposition/What it's all about). Begin with the problem or obstacle your character needs to change. Her first line is prompted by the other person's words or deeds that propel your character to embark on her journey. Her need is urgent and of life-and-death importance, immediately compelling the audience to care about your character, and connect with her ideas and what she needs to achieve. Choose the specific sensory needs to create her environment and the world she inhabits. Begin your journey using a focused simplicity to clearly express her emotional needs.

Act II (The Middle: Story/The how). Express your chosen arguments to the other person. Justifying why he should support and help you reach your objective will unearth discoveries and reactions to aid you in winning him over. The discoveries and events made during her monologue offers your character new avenues for achieving her objective. Reactions from the other person cause a light bulb to go on in your character's head, revealing new realizations regarding her situation, circumstance, or new dimensions in the other person. It becomes clear to her and to the audience what is important.

Act III (The Resolution: End). The discoveries create growth and emotional changes. Heightening your awareness of the importance of the other person allows your character to know if she has achieved her objective. Whether she achieves it or not, or decides to remain where she is, your character is now in a different emotional place and ready to move on with her life.

Edmund

Act I

Edmund's first act is direct and clearly focused. Hearing his father, the Earl of Gloucester, tell the Earl of Kent of the embarrassment of Edmund's presence and his imminent exile propels Edmund into immediate action.

> *Thou, Nature, art my goddess; to thy law my services are bound. Wherefore should I stand in the plague of custom, and permit the curiosity of nations to deprive me, for that I am some twelve or fourteen moonshines lag of a brother? Why bastard?*

He sets up his commitment and posits the question plaguing him. These words, spoken for the first time, awaken Edmund to his need for embarking on his long sought after acceptance. He presents his need for Nature's impartiality to end his plague-ridden voices.

Act II

Edmund justifies his beliefs.

> *Wherefore base, when my dimensions are as well compact, my mind as generous, and my shape as true, as honest madam's issue? Why brand they us with base? with baseness? bastardy? base, base? Who, in the lusty stealth of nature, take more composition and fierce quality than doth, within dull,*

> *stale, tired bed, go to th' creating a whole tribe of*
> *fops got 'tween asleep and wake? Well then,*
> *Legitimate Edgar, I must have your land. Our*
> *father's love is to the bastard Edmund as to th'*
> *legitimate. Fine word, "legitimate"!*

He presents his case for deserving equality with Edgar. Comparing the facts of his exciting birth to the dullness and ordinariness of Edgar's, he presents his case for deserving his father's title and estate. He allows Nature and the audience to understand his reasoning. There is no reason for Gloucester's dalliance to be held against Edmund.

Act III
In resolution, Edmund opens up to Nature.

> *Well, my legitimate, if this letter speed and my*
> *invention thrive, Edmund the base shall top th'*
> *legitimate. I grow, I prosper Now, gods, stand up*
> *for bastards!*

Edmund feels the heat of Nature's glow leading him to triumph. She has understood. Edmund is convinced Nature has directed him to move forward with his plan. He caresses the letter. This all-important letter will change his life.

Serafina

Act I
Serafina's first act begins with background information and a need to respond to Flora's response about her envy toward the women's planned trip to New Orleans.

> *My folks was peasants, contadini, but he—he*
> *come from land-owners! Signorille, my husband!*
> *—At night I sit here and I'm satisfied to remember,*
> *because I had the best. —Not the third best and not*

> *the second best, but the* first *best, the* only *best!—*
> *So now I stay here and am satisfied now to*
> *remember, ...*

Serafina informs Flora and Bessie that she and Rosario shared a
love that comes once in a lifetime, and that she is satisfied to
remain the grieving Sicilian Catholic widow.

Act II
Serafina justifies her desire to stay with Rosario.

> *I count up the nights I held him all night in my*
> *arms, and I can tell you how many. Each night for*
> *twelve years. Four thousand—three hundred—*
> *and eighty. The number of nights I held him all*
> *night in my arms. Sometimes I didn't sleep, just*
> *held him all night in my arms. And I am satisfied*
> *with it. I grieve for him. Yes, my pillow at night's*
> *never dry—but I'm satisfied to remember. And I*
> *would feel cheap and degraded and not fit to live*
> *with my daughter or under the roof with the urn*
> *of his blessed ashes, those—ashes of a rose—if*
> *after that memory, after knowing that man, I*
> *went to some other, some middle-aged man, not*
> *young, not full of young passion, but getting a pot*
> *belly on him and losing his hair and smelling of*
> *sweat and liquor—and trying to fool myself that*
> *that was love-making!*

She explains her choice to live in the past. She knows the exact
number of nights they had together. She is locked into this memory. She will never look at another man because of Rosa. It is
important to set the proper example for Rosa. A wild passionate
woman can calm the fires forever once she has experienced great
sex and love. Besides, who would be out there for her except
unworthy drunken bores.

Act III

Serafina ends her explanation to Flora and Bessie by protesting she is satisfied to live with memories.

> I know *what love-making was. And I'm satisfied just to remember... Go on, you do it, you go on the streets and let them drop their sacks of dirty water on you!—I'm satisfied to remember the love of a man that was mine*—only mine! *Never touched by the hand of* nobody! Nobody *but me!—Just* me! *Never nobody but me!*

Rosario is the great love and passion for Serafina, the fulfillment of what she had in her life, she accepts living with her memories. She chooses to remain the grieving, ever-loving Sicilian widow.

Beneatha

Act I

Beneatha's first act is short. It consists of only two one-word questions, one three-word statement, and one one-word statement prompted by Asagai's concern for her new situation and his question about her present.

> *Me?... Me?... Me, I'm nothing ... Me.*

Beneath's six-word response draws her out of her numb and paralyzed emotional state. It is the beginning of emotional movement and requires the necessary time to answer Asagai. This is the first time in her life she has not had answers at her fingertips. She wants Asagai to understand the importance of her feelings about herself.

She is safe at home, and that allows her to explore her feelings to Asagai.

Act II

Beneatha justifies her feelings about herself by sharing her story with Asagai.

When I was very small... we used to take our sleds out in the wintertime and the only hills we had were the ice-covered stone steps of some houses down the street. And we used to fill them in with snow and make them smooth and slide down them all day... and it was very dangerous, you know... far too steep... and sure enough one day a kid named Rufus came down too fast and hit the sidewalk and we saw his face just split open right there in front of us... And I remember standing there looking at his bloody open face thinking that was the end of Rufus. But the ambulance came and they took him to the hospital and they fixed the broken bones and they sewed it all up... and the next time I saw Rufus he just had a little line down the middle of his face... I never got over that ... That that was what one person could do for another, fix him up—sew up the problem, make him all right again. That was the most marvelous thing in the world... I wanted to do that. I always thought it was the one concrete thing in the world that a human being could do. Fix up the sick, you know—and make them whole again. This was truly being God... I wanted to cure.

Beneatha reveals the origin of her dreams and discovers her feelings anew in these moments with Asagai. As she relates this story, she reawakens her feelings of the powers of science and medicine, and her belief in their contribution to humanity. She discovers the importance her dreams hold for her.

Act III
Beneatha arrives at a pained resolution, needing Asagai's guidance.

It used to be so important to me. I wanted to cure. It used to matter. I used to care. I mean about people and how their bodies hurt . . . it doesn't seem deep enough, close enough to what ails mankind! It was a child's way of seeing things—or an idealist's.

Beneatha comes to realize a deeper and more profound importance of her dream. The outlook for achieving her dream is bleak. She cannot go there. She protects herself. She covers the truth with cynicism. For now.

Peter

Act I
Peter's first act is a short, indirectly direct prologue using his ironic sense of humor to reach Heidi.

What a perky Seventies kind of gal you are! You can separate sexual needs from emotional dependencies. Heidi, if you tell me you secrete endorphins when you run, I'm going straight intothe curator's office and demand an all armor retrospective.

Heidi's declaration of her newfound ability to compartmentalize her physical and emotional needs horrifies Peter into a response. Standing outside the Chicago Art Institute, he adjusts to the outdoor space and the many people around him. He has a keen sense of how to get her attention.

Act II
Peter justifies his fears about Heidi's lack of emotional commitment to her life by sharing his own commitment with her.

Actually, I'm afraid I'm feeling sort of distant from you. I'm not criticizing you. It's just how I'm feeling. I haven't seen you in eight months. Heidi, I don't play on your team. I've become a liberal homosexual pediatrician. And I prefer Stanley. My

*friend's name is Stanley Zinc. He's a child psychi-
atrist from Johns Hopkins. But he's thinking of
quitting in order to study with Merce Cunningham. The sad thing is that Stanley is too old to
join the company and Miss Merce isn't getting any
younger, either. Anyway, I'm thinking of replacing
him with a waiter I met last week, we share a
mutual distrust of Laura Nyro. I would have told
you all this earlier but I thought we deserved
something more intimate than a phone call. So I
chose the Chicago Art Institute.*

Once he has her attention he proceeds with his true feelings
toward her, revealing for the first time his emotional life with
Stanley Zinc, including the joys and annoyances of emotional
commitment. Humorously, he shares with Heidi the importance
of emotional attachment to another human being.

Act III
Peter arrives at a place where he realizes Heidi's preoccupation
does not allow her to hear anything he has said.

*Heidi, I'm gay, okay? I sleep with Stanley Zinc,
M.D. And my liberation, my pursuit of happiness,
and the pursuit of happiness of other men like
me is just as politically and socially valid as
hanging a couple of Goddamned paintings
because they were signed by someone named
Nancy, Gladys, or Gilda. And that is why I came
to see you today. I am demanding your equal
time and consideration.*

Peter, in a mixture of humor and hurt fury, lays his objective out
in the open for Heidi to hear. He wants the same respect, consideration, and confirmation she is willing to give her work and her
causes. He needs to feel important in her life and wants her to
know and accept him.

Turning your monologue into a three-act play brings focus and simplicity to your work. It allows you to fully understand your character's emotional journey, bringing the freedom and spontaneity to commit yourself to your choices and believe in your character's needs and life.

10

Performing Your Work

Performing your work at this stage will yield information you can use to fill in any missing links in your character's emotional life. After incorporating all the tools and specifically fulfilling each of the character's needs, you arrive at the moment to test drive your work.

At this point in your process, everything will not run smoothly. The point is to see what is working properly, what is not working and what is missing. You are familiar with your choices and decisions. They are not yet second nature. They will not yet fit like a second skin. That is not what you are investigating at this time by performing your work. Remember you are performing the work you have done up to this time. There is more to be done. This is a plateau you have reached where performing the work will yield information. Don't look for results. They will be shaky at best. Don't judge yourself or your work.

Performing your work at this time in the process is investigative. It is more important to find out what is working than what is not. Don't belabor the moments that are not working. You are not far enough along in your process for it all to work. Much to your surprise, more will work than won't. The information guides you in knowing what is missing, what needs to be corrected or changed. It is only the moments that jump out at you that need to be explored before you go on.

Investigate the reasons you made your decision. Examine your justifications for that decision. You have come a long way, and the familiarity you have with your character will assist you in learning where things are really off. This is not just to point out where you are off in your performance skills. Enjoy your work. Perform it to the fullest. Remember, you are only test driving your character. Don't look for perfection. This is one step in your process. It is an information-seeking quest for what you have achieved thus far. Fly by the seat of your pants. Let go of your work. Jump out of the plane without a parachute and watch yourself soar. Believe in the work you have done up to this point. Commit to your choices. You will learn the truth of where you are and where you need to delve deeper.

Beginning with the Moment Before

The moment before needs to be built into your character's foundation. The moment before is the emotional moment just before beginning to speak. The moment before prepares you to begin where your character is emotionally living in the moment. The situation that describes your character's emotional life begins prior to her first word.

Your character is alive before you meet her. Her monologue begins with her moment before. Your preparation involves sensory externals and emotional realities that transport you into your character's psyche. Allow your character to experience her environment, clothing, and inner dialogue in her moment before.

The moment before is specifically the emotional state in which your character lives, in the moment before beginning her monologue, not the time, day, or hour before. Building the specific moment is very important. Taking the needed time to create the moment before transports you under your character's skin. You begin inhabiting her the exact moment before and start to experience her reactions to her situation and circumstance, building her emotional state in the moment.

Feelings aren't facts. They are feelings, sometimes based solely on the ephemera of life's moments. Don't analyze them. Experience them. Live in them. Allow them to affect you. This brings them into your character's existence.

The moment before is not the time to go over your lines, actions, beats, or any of the work. Trust in your work. Believe in the choices you have made and commit yourself to fulfilling each action to reach your character's objective. The moment before belongs to your character. Begin sharing yourself. The goal of building the moment before is to get under her skin and into her soul. The strongest and quickest way to accomplish getting there is using your senses. Begin by recreating your character's sensory reality and truth. Now dive into the moment before.

Edmund

Edmund's moment before recalls Gloucester's feelings of embarrassment, caused by Edmund's very presence. Gloucester's announcement of Edmund's banishment strikes him like a whiplash. He has just returned. Now he is to be sent away again.

He cannot stop the flood of emotional pain surging at him. Conflicted thoughts rush into his mind. He tries to combat this massive torrent. The lightbulb of discovery goes on and through this surging of pain comes an idea. He quickly gets a piece of parchment. In this emotional state, he composes his letter. Words pour forth. He writes the letter to his father.

He finishes and reads it. Doubts begin to creep into his mind. His indictment of Edgar appears to be his only option. His inner conflict drives him against Edgar. To proceed or not to proceed hammers in his brain.

He needs affirmation. Who can he turn to? Nature is fair and impartial, believing all people are equal and not judged by the origins of their birth.

These events create his heightened emotional state. They need to be experienced and built into Edmund's moment before. He is highly charged but needs to appear rational and clearheaded.

Find an experience in your life when you felt rejected, unloved, ridiculed. Explore these feelings. Examine the thoughts careening through your mind. The sensations raging in your body. The acuteness of your pain, a moment so blinding you feel the need to lash out.

This is the first time Edmund allows himself to live with this unbearable pain. His nine years away have softened the edge of these feelings. His father's words have brought them tumbling back, only this time with a need to stop them for all time. Added to this feeling of pain comes anger against his legitimate brother.

Build Edmund's moment before specifically, one sensory and emotional truth at a time. This makes it real, visceral, and unbearable. This emotional unbearability is where Edmund begins.

Serafina

Serafina's moment before is multilayered: physical activities, emotional situations, internal seeking and searching all at once. She's looking for the Bulova watch, getting herself together to go to Rosa's graduation, and being forced to both finish Flora's blouse and listen to the women's mindless chatter. All are elements involved in building a truthful and specific moment before for Serafina. The three years since Rosario's death have not dulled her sense of loss. It has grown stronger and deeper. Now, in her emotionally almost paralytic state and wearing her mourning like a shroud, she is propelled to leave the house. This is the first time she will be in public since her tragic loss.

Her love for Rosa and the importance of getting to the graduation on time are driving forces in her moment before. She is desperate to discover where she hid Rosa's graduation present. In the same moment, she is figuring out what to wear to the graduation to make her appearance pleasing to Rosa. Add to her moment before the need to finish the already paid for ugly blouse.

All of the above needs to be layered into Serafina's moment before. This totality will create a strongly defined and specific moment before preparing her to fulfill her monologue.

Recall a time when you felt like the living dead. It is a state of depression almost debilitating, a sensation like walking through water. This adjustment to Serafina's emotional state needs to be strongly layered into her moment before.

Physically search your own home for something you need immediately. Experience the building urgency as the moments tick by. Explore the feelings of anxiety and frustration.

Enhance this with the need to get someplace important on time. A place you need to look your best and be in control of yourself. The anxiety you normally feel on your way to an audition can be used for Serafina's angst about going out in public and facing the other mothers. Recreate the feelings of fear of failing, the joy of performing, and experiencing the judgement.

Combining these elements into building Serafina's complex moment before will bring strong feelings, immediacy, and urgency. It will emotionally place Serafina in the emotional state to spew forth her declarations and protestations of love and satisfaction.

Beneatha

Beneatha's moment before begins with Bobo's announcement of the loss of the money. She is existing with numb and defeated sensations about this turn of events. Asagai's question causes her to confront herself.

Beneatha's dreams, which allowed her to live a life of escape, have shattered like glass. She is experiencing her uncovered self for the first time. She is brand new to herself, unable to hide in front of Asagai.

This immediacy creates new feelings of emptiness. Without her protective shell of humor and cynicism, she is forced to face the truth of the moment, openly and vulnerably.

Find a moment in your life when you experienced emotional and spiritual devastation: when you felt bereft of everything that made your life full and rich, content, and bursting with opportunity, a moment you were alone and hopeless, when you felt your life was over and were unable to think of any possibility for your future.

Explore your state of mind in this moment. Delve into these feelings through your senses. Feel them. Taste and smell them. Let them exist throughout your body. Bring them into Beneatha. Use the sensory path to build her moment before.

Go to a moment you were sure you were going to get the role of your heart's desire, the role that was going to change your life forever. Open yourself to the instant you heard you did not get the part. Reawaken the specific thoughts that went through your head. The feelings that pummeled your psyche and beat you down. Stay in those feelings of the moment.

It has been an hour since Beneatha has heard the news. Her numbness has had time to engulf her like a thick fog. She can hardly breathe. She has no desire to breathe. She wants time to stop, to reverse itself. This is the state of emotional truth needed to build Beneatha's specific and intricate moment before.

Peter

Peter's moment before is one of complexity and discovery and begins with his hurt feelings from Heidi's phone call. During the time it takes him to get to her, his pain has multiplied and been joined by anger. When he sees her and experiences her preoccupation, outrage, horror, and concern are stirred into the mix of his already overripe emotions. He is appalled at the Heidi standing in front of him.

Revive a personal moment when a close friend left you nonplussed. The reason is not important. The emotional truth and its effects are. Add the feelings you experience when a friend treats you inconsiderately, taking you for granted. The hurt mixes with anger and frustration. Toss in a moment when you felt indifference and needed understanding. Now spend time with these feelings. Allow them to simmer as they do for Peter as he travels to see Heidi.

Peter's moment before also needs care and concern for Heidi. He is appalled at her emotional compartmentalization and at the same time scared for her. Add in his complicated and confused emotional state about his homosexuality.

Choose the most important and meaningful relationship in your life. Find a moment in that relationship when it appeared it was ending. Explore your feelings in that moment. Recreate the sensations it brought up. Bring these sensory experiences to Peter.

Examine and accept what you dislike about yourself. Explore your feelings in the moment of acceptance. Relive these feelings. Recreate them to add them one at a time in building Peter's multilayered and complex moment before.

Diving into the moment before one emotional aspect at a time will transport you into the truth and reality of your character's life and soul, preparing you to be in the precisely needed emotional state to begin his monologue.

Living Each Moment for the First Time

Each moment is happening in the moment and needs to be lived for the first time. It eliminates your character's ability to protect herself from the other person. Living each moment for the first time takes courage. Each moment is new. Your character is saying the words for the first time. This is a paramount need in keeping her alive in the moment and eliminating anticipation. No moment is like any other in life. There may be similarities, but each is different and new.

Living in the moment for the first time has a strong and definite impact. Each moment needs to be created for the first time. Never repeat moments. Recreate anew. Repeating dulls their sensations, robotizes them, places them on automatic pilot.

The first time makes it a fresh and new experience. Every action, word, and emotional response is lived fully for the first time.

Edmund

Edmund calls on Nature for the first time. He may have talked to her before but not on this spot, in this climate, and certainly not about this matter. These elements make it a first-time experience.

> *Thou, Nature, art my goddess; to thy law my services are bound.*

This is the first time he expresses total commitment to her. The first time he acknowledges her omnipotence. He is cautious and trepidatious because it is new territory. He is putting himself in a vulnerable position by asking for help and support. She might reject his plan.

This is the first time he has spoken so explicitly in comparing himself to legitimate Edgar. The first time he has dared to utter aloud his right to share his father's love, title, and property. He has had some of these thoughts before but never voiced them. Living in the moment for the first time, Edmund is unable to anticipate Nature's reaction.

This lack of anticipatory knowledge allows him to experience triumph for the first time.

> *Edmund the base shall top th' legitimate. I grow, I prosper.*

Edmund is now a new man living in a new skin. With Nature in his corner, he is supported and ready to face the challenges that lie in front of him. Not knowing what they are allows him to experience each moment for the first time.

Serafina

Serafina has spoken with Flora before, but this is the first time she shares intimacies about her relationship with Rosario. Because of Flora's suggestion that she end her mourning and reenter the world, Serafina feels compelled to open up to her for the first time and share her reasons for choosing to remain in the past.

> *I had the best.—Not the third best and not the second best, but the* first *best, the* only *best!*

As she declares the quality of their love and lovemaking, she reawakens in the moment to her loss and what she is missing. Her emotional and sexual desires grow as she becomes more immersed and emphatic in reliving her truth. This is the first time she has allowed herself to rekindle and reexperience the depth of her feelings.

For the first time, Serafina allows herself to fantasize about the kind of man awaiting her. She finds herself amused by her image.

> *. . . some middle-aged man, not young, not full of young passion, but getting a pot belly on him and losing his hair and smelling of sweat and liquor . . . .*

This image, expressed for the first time, seals her fate, binding her to the past more deeply than before.

Beneatha

Beneatha lives for the first time with a loss of herself. This is the first time she has not been in control of her future and the first time she is not filled with the promise of a wonderful and exciting future.

She tries to answer Asagai's question and for the first time finds herself without words. Her only response is a repetition of his question.

Me?

This is the first time she has no answer about herself. She is strongly affected by her response.

Me?

The effect of this awareness creates a stronger paralysis of thought. Living this new experience, she repeats the question again with even greater rising fear. Fighting against the oncoming torrent of pain, she forces herself to move forward.

Me, I'm nothing.

Arriving at a word to express herself she is amazed at the profound effect of Walter Lee's actions. For the first time, she experiences pain and vulnerability created by being tossed into the abyss of uncertainly and hopelessness. She is experiencing every breath for the first time and allows nothing in but the air she breathes.

As she recalls Rufus' story and reawakens to her discovery of her calling to the medical profession, she recreates this experience with fresh eyes. As she proceeds, moment by moment, she feels she is being born again. She recognizes these were the dreams of a child. She now begins to embrace them as an adult. Believing for the first time she may not be able to fulfill her dreams, she lashes out at herself.

It was a child's way of seeing things—or an idealist's.

She now sees a need to change these views, move forward with them, and find a way to realize them as a newly born adult.

Peter

Peter experiences this new Heidi for the first time, which compels him to blurt out his instinctual and instantaneous response.

> *What a perky Seventies kind of gal you are! You can separate sexual needs from emotional dependencies.*

This is the first time Peter has felt the need to lash out at her and penetrate her protective shell.

> *Actually, I'm afraid I'm feeling sort of distant from you. I'm not criticizing you. It's just how I'm feeling.*

He expresses his immediate feelings. This is the first time he has not felt connected to Heidi. His need is to mend their separation. Heidi's reactions propel him to share his truth for the first time.

> *I've become a liberal homosexual pediatrician. And I prefer Stanley. My friend's name is Stanley Zinc.*

This new information reveals his true self. He hopes to get Heidi to pay attention to him, but instead, she receives his news with no reaction. He tries again.

> *Heidi, I'm gay, okay?*

Again, Heidi does not respond. Peter now demands her attention for the first time in their relationship.

> *I am demanding your equal time and consideration.*

Heidi's indifference and lack of response to his personal information justifies his need to demand her to hear him.

Living in the moment for the first time brings your character's emotional life to a tingling aliveness: informing the other person of what is important, allowing her to understand new facets and aspects of their relationship, experiencing his needs from the other person for the first time.

Each character expresses herself in her own personal way, living with the sensations of experiencing the moment for the first time.

The first time creates a visceral awareness needed to prompt change, accept defeat, or remain in the same emotional place with obstacles intact. No matter which of these results comes, the actions of living each moment for the first time create the strongest and most deeply felt truth.

Eliminating Anticipation

Living each moment for the first time eliminates anticipation. You know your character's story. You have worked out each beat, action, and event in his life. You even know his future and the outcome regarding his objective. Now comes the hard part—leaving that knowledge behind.

Eliminating anticipation requires faith, belief, and commitment. It takes a leap of faith to live in your character's present for the first time. Faith that if you let go of your work, it will be there when you need it. Belief you did the right work and enough of it. And commitment to fulfilling each and every moment and action. This leap into the unknown is what causes fear and anxiety. Let go, jump in, and enjoy the result of all your intricate work.

Anticipation belies that the moment is happening for the first time. It occurs when the actor's knowledge enters the character's psyche. Your character can't anticipate future events if she is living in the moment. Keeping your character truthful and honest to her circumstances and situation preclude knowing what happens in the next moment, let alone anything that happens in her future. Anticipation destroys the truth and honesty of your character. You live with anticipation of the outcome of an action, but you have no knowledge of what will happen. You can only imagine the outcome.

Anticipation informs in advance. Stay in the moment. Experience your character's life for the first time. Committing to your choices, letting go of your work, and inhabiting your character's existence eliminate any possibility of anticipation.

Anticipation makes your job harder. It softens the pain, eases the blow, and eliminates any possibility of surprise or mystery. It shortchanges you, depriving you of the visceral experience of the moment and causing you to manufacture feelings and reactions.

Turn yourself over to your character's soul and psyche. Trust and believe in your work. Totally commit to inhabiting your character, and you will eliminate anticipation.

Edmund

Edmund knows there will be repercussions from his actions but blinds himself to them. His imagination fantasizes, but he has no knowledge of the specifics. He stays in the moment and experiences each event as it happens. He doesn't know if Nature will affirm his wishes. She may strike him down for what he is planning. He has no idea how Gloucester will respond to the letter; he may not believe it was written by Edgar.

Moment by moment, event by event, Edmund lives in the moment, believing in his plan and moving forward with no foreknowledge of Nature's response.

Serafina

Serafina is choosing to live in the past and not allowing the future into her life. She cannot anticipate what is to come.

She lives her choice. Holding onto her past and refusing to move forward, she cannot anticipate what Fate may have in store for her. Serafina is unable to anticipate or predict Alvaro's arrival.

Beneatha

Beneatha could not anticipate Walter's Lee's action. She would have tried to prevent it if she could have. She would never have allowed him to take away her future. Forced to live in the moment without future knowledge, the news hits her like a ton of bricks. She fights against believing the truth until it permeates her being. The effect is so powerful, she remains in the same numb and empty emotional state. She hides from any thoughts of the future. Holding tight to the present prevents anticipation.

Peter

It is impossible for Peter to anticipate the density of Heidi's indifference. She is a revelation to him. He experiences Heidi anew in each moment. By eliminating anticipation, he is struck dumb by the effect of Heidi's behavior. Allowing himself to live in this moment without anticipating the future, he is forced to strike out at Heidi like a wounded animal. Anticipating would ameliorate Peter's reaction, soften the blow, minimize his reactions. He has no time to anticipate how Heidi will behave in the coming moments or what the consequences of his actions may be.

The value of eliminating anticipation should be clear. Your ability to take this leap of faith brings excitement and truth to your work. Take the chance. Make this choice. Fly by the seat of your pants. It brings a multitude of rewards to you and your audience.

Taking Your Time with Transitions

Taking your time with transitions allows them to happen organically. A transition is a change from one emotion to another, moving you from one action to the next. Transitions take time. Allow your character to experience each moment and action truthfully by taking the time needed to make the change.

Transitions are prompted by an internal thought. They may be motivated by an action or word from the other person. They may occur from a look you get. A discovery can prompt a transition. Transitions need to be made clearly, one step at a time, until they are fully completed. Transitions require time, time to emotionally live through all the steps needed to communicate the change simply and clearly.

Transitions also happen when making decisions, discoveries, or anything prompting an emotional change in your character. Allow your character to be affected by the need to make the transition. It is important for you to fulfill her need to experience these moments.

Take the necessary time to go from one moment to the next. Do not rush through transitions. Rushing clouds moments communicating confusion. Trust that taking the time to fulfill the transition will hold the other person in rapt attention until you fully reach the next moment. Taking the needed time eliminates anticipation and keeps you alive and in the moment.

Edmund

Edmund calls upon Nature and informs her of his allegiance.

> *... to thy law my services are bound.*

Certain he has her attention, he makes a transition to the issue he needs her help with.

> *Wherefore should I*
> *Stand in the plague of custom, and permit*
> *The curiosity of nations to deprive me,*
> *For that I am some twelve or fourteen moonshines*
> *Lag of a brother?*

This transition may take only a breath, but that breath needs its time. By taking this beat, Edmund is clearly in the moment to begin his quest for her help. He had no idea how he would ask for her help. He discovered the words in the moment without any anticipation after he made the transition to this beat.

> *Why bastard? Wherefore base,*

Another transition to what plagues him, what drives him to ask for help. It is a circumstance of his life he needs to correct. Allow him to take his time to make the transition and arrive in the next moment. This drives him through his monologue.

Serafina

Serafina is talking to Flora and Bessie. When she tries to explain what her relationship with Rosario was about, she begins at the beginning.

> *My folks was peasants, contadini, but he—he come from land-owners!*

She takes a beat, defined by the dash, before going on. That dash is a breath, it allows her to remember vividly her life in Sicily as a young girl and the first moment she laid eyes on the handsome Rosario. She needs time to take in all of this in that breath. She needs to fulfill this transition. Take the time needed, and fully experience his image. Then make the transition to the next beat. Give yourself the time to fully explore her sensations in the moment.

> *So now I stay here and am satisfied now to remember, . . . I count up the nights I held him all night in my arms, and I can tell you how many.*

In this part of her speech, she takes a beat defined by the ellipses to decide what next to tell them. This can be a short beat or a deep breath. Use the needed time to transition fully to the next beat. Each beat is equally important.

Again, this process eliminates anticipation, letting Serafina live each moment for the first time.

Beneatha

Beneatha begins her monologue with great difficulty. She finds it impossible to answer Asagai's question. Her response is,

> *Me? . . . Me? . . . Me, I'm nothing . . . Me.*

Her first is a question, then a pause, the ellipses, in which she thinks about herself. Again, she is unable to come up with a thought. She takes another pause, the ellipses, this time fighting off the truth of her feelings. Finally, she is forced to reveal her truth in the moment. She answers Asagai's inquiry with honesty. These are emotionally very difficult moments for her. She needs to take the time in each pause to search for an answer to his question. Each pause needs to be a fully realized transition before moving to the next beat. These transitional moments display her emotional state in the moment. Beneatha has never been short on words. Because this is a first for her, she needs the requisite amount of time to search her soul for an answer.

Another moment where Beneatha makes a strong transition is when she says,

> *That was the most marvelous thing in the world...*
> *I wanted to do that.*

These ellipses represent her unwillingness to reveal her truth. Take the time to live in this transition. Allow it to express her difficulty in speaking her idealistic truth. It is a discovery she unearths from her subconscious. Help her by giving her the time to allow in the truth. A big moment is coming back to her as she tells Asagai of her lost innocence.

Peter

Peter begins talking to Heidi in a state of emotional fury. He tries using humor to lessen the blow but realizes he needs to cool down and speak from honest feelings not anger. He takes the moment to regain his composure. He needs to take his time to make the transition to defuse his anger and move on to express his truth in the moment.

> *Actually, I'm afraid I'm feeling sort of distant from*
> *you.*

By taking his time to make his emotional transitions, he succeeds in getting her to pay attention to him for a moment.

Later in the monologue, he tells of his life's decision and Stanley, the man he shares his life with. He follows his personal revelation with wry humor to lighten the weight of his revelations.

> *I would have told you all this earlier but I thought*
> *we deserved something more intimate than a*
> *phone call. So I chose the Chicago Art Institute.*

He needs the moment to change tones completely. None of this is coming easy for him, as glib as he appears. His glibness has always been his means of cover and protection. He understands fully the power of humor and its effects on an emotionally heavy expression of truth. He takes his cue from Heidi's reactions.

Transitions come in varying forms. They all need the required amount of time to make them real. Each transition needs to be fully realized, offering clarity and understanding of your character's truth and honesty. Time allows transitions to live in each moment for the first time.

Taking your time with transitions carries your audience along on your character's emotional journey.

11

Connecting the Dots

Putting It All Together

Connecting the dots is one of the more interesting puzzles children play. In front of them is a page filled with a maze of numbered dots. They are to connect one dot to the next in numerical order, beginning at number one and continuing until they reach the last numbered dot. At this point, a completely defined face emerges from the maze, a face that includes eyes, mouth, nose, and sometimes even ears.

At the start of the journey, children have no idea what the finished face will turn out to be, but by diligently, simply, and specifically connecting the dots, this fully realized face appears right before their eyes. There is no anticipation of the result or second-guessing the outcome. They just took the journey from start to finish trusting and believing the result would bring them a satisfying reward.

Putting together all the pieces of the road map rewards you with a complex, fully realized person. It's one step at a time. The primary difference between the two processes is that when connecting the dots, the children had a piece of paper in front of them and pencils in their hand. It was tangible. When you are putting all your choices and decisions together and connecting them, it is subjective. You are on the inside and can't see the person emerge. By trusting your instincts and insights that led you to each choice and decision, you have the opportunity to see if connecting the dots of your work creates a three-dimensional human being.

Putting it all together begins with a rehearsal of your mono-logue. The rehearsal is to put your road map to use. Connect the dots to fulfill your monologue. To get the most out of your rehearsal, I suggest you begin by deciding on the appropriate amount of time you feel is right for you. That time is determined by the amount of time you are able to concentrate, the amount of time you feel you can work your monologue, remain alert, and keep the work fresh. Thirty to forty-five minutes per monologue is usually the right amount of time. Be methodical and disci-plined. Set this time aside for your rehearsal. Write it in your appointment book or personal diary. Make it a part of your day. Doing it daily yields the best results. But you know yourself, so choose a routine that will work for you.

Use your kitchen timer; if you don't have one, purchase one. It will prove invaluable to your process and in other areas of your work and life. It does three- or four-minute eggs perfectly. Set the timer for your chosen time. If you are going to bake a potato, set it for forty-five minutes. When it pings, your work is done and you can sit down and enjoy your potato. That's multitasking without distracting from your work.

Do nothing except work on your monologue during this allotted time. No phone calls. No eating. Nothing! If you find yourself resistant, sit down but do nothing else. This time is ded-icated to your work. After a time, your frustration level will build, and you will find yourself working. Once you begin work-ing, you will start to enjoy yourself and feel a sense of satisfac-tion akin to Serafina's.

Begin your process by building your character's moment before. During your first few rehearsals, you may not successfully fulfill this segment of your work before the timer pings. This is okay. Building the moment before is an important and very neces-sary part of your process. It is the starting point. It sets your char-acter on the correct path toward his emotional journey. Rushing into the monologue without satisfactorily fulfilling the moment before will create doubt about your work. It will cause you to alter your choices, actions, or adjustments before you have truly had a chance to feel them work. Don't be hasty. Fulfill your character's moment before. Get him off on the right path and proceed.

When you are ready, begin to rehearse the work you have done on your monologue. If you feel a glitch—a moment that is not organically flowing into the next, an awkward feeling, or a transition that seems wrong—make a note of it and continue. Do not stop to solve the problem; continue with your monologue. Sometimes moments or transitions that don't work clear themselves up if you move forward. The next beat may clarify the last one.

Allow yourself to find all the problems first. In another rehearsal period, you can begin the problem-solving part of your work by attacking problems one at a time. Reaching the end of your monologue brings satisfaction. It also informs you of the many choices and decisions you have made and guides you on how to proceed in your next rehearsal.

The next most important value of setting the timer is hearing it ping, announcing you have come to the end of your work time. When the ping goes off, end your work for that day. Do not continue working. Do not overwork. Stop working at the ping. Don't binge work, that is, work until you are exhausted or bored with what you are doing. Overdoing it will cause you to resist getting back to your work on a regular basis in a disciplined fashion. You may wind up not coming back to your work for days, sometimes even weeks. Slow and steady yields the best results. Remember the fable of the tortoise and the hare.

If the ping sounds when you find you are on a roll and coming up with new and inventive ideas, write them down. But stop. Stopping is one of the most important parts of any creative process. Working for three hours at a time prevents you from coming back to it the next day or even the next. You will hear yourself saying, "I don't have three hours." This is the truth. But you can always find thirty or forty-five minutes for your work. This method of consistent and diligent work builds a solid foundation. If you choose to go on, you will find diminishing results.

Begin the next rehearsal by perusing your notes from your last rehearsal. These notes will stimulate your creative juices and bring you back into the life of your character. You'll be creatively right where you ended. If you don't believe this or have doubts, try it. Give it a shot, and see for yourself.

Less is more. A shorter amount of time fully concentrated on a regular basis yields more results than a longer amount of time creating resistance and a cloudy head when you finally stop.

Once you have gotten through your monologue and have a few beats that felt wrong or mistaken, go back and take a look at them. You may have to adjust some of your choices or change others. You may discover you have not taken the time necessary to make the proper transition. This last is major. Taking your time can result in exciting moments you didn't even know were there. Explore taking your time. You will know when you are taking too long. Your character will have nothing to do. Don't act too hastily. Give it another try before you jump to changing things. Remember, all of this is new, and like a new pair of shoes you have to wear them in before they become comfortable. Your work in developing your character is like a baby learning to walk. At first, the baby teeters and falls over. The next time he will take a few steps and then a few more until it feels right. So it is with living in your character's skin.

Completing each of the steps on your road map leads to the fulfillment of your character and her or his monologue. It supports you in performing your monologue without thinking about the work. The work is the actor's tool. It is not in the consciousness of the character. Make your choices. Fulfill each one, and enjoy yourself as you soar into your character's consciousness.

Your road map frees you to live in the moment and offers you total spontaneity. You can change the order, moving each step around freely until you find the process that works for you. The important thing is to fulfill each item. Using your road map creates a complex character performing a compelling monologue.

Checking Your Road Map

Checking your road map will ensure that all your work has been done. Use it as a guide. It consists of a simple connecting-the-dots list of steps.

- Choose a monologue.
- Plumb your text.

- Interpret your monologue from the subjective point of view.
- Use your acting tools.
- Lay out your character's emotional journey.
- Break down your script.
- Inhabit your character.
- Create and believe in the other person.
- Shape your monologue into a three-act play.
- Perform your work.
- Connect the dots.